"Cere Demuth's book *THE* .... than *A Memoir Of Recovery*'. It is a thrilling intimate book of family survival that is impossible to put down. Born into the era of peace and love, Cere's story, as a daughter; wife; mother and grandmother takes us into the chaos of that era, it's aftermath and the power of drug addiction to ruin everything it touches. Told in a brilliant mixture of prose and poetry. A gripping and harrowing story that will have you falling in love with the characters and praying for them all to find peace and happiness."

—Country Joe McDonald,
Singer/Songwriter, Author, Activist

"*THE WAY WE STAY: A Memoir of Recovery* by Cere Demuth shines a spotlight on how interwoven pain and love can be. Her tale, a mother with a heroin-addicted son, *THE WAY WE STAY* is told with a stark, poignant fragility. A story of one woman's heartbreak. A story meant for the world. A story you won't want to put down."

—Susan Wingate, Amazon bestseller,
award-winning author, www.susanwingate.com

"I went into this memoir expecting to relate on some level to the pain and struggle a family endured watching a beloved member struggle with addiction, but I received so much more. A raw, powerful, emotional journey that embraces motherhood, being a daughter, a wife, and a woman. *The Way We Stay* made me step back and left me examining my own life, taking a deep breath, and being honest..."

—Barb Lord, Book Reviewer @_thatswhatsheread

"It must have taken so much courage to share this incredible story. I read it in one day - I couldn't put it down. It's *real, raw, and honest*. For those of us that know and love an addict - it will speak to you on a deep level while giving you hope."

—Amazon.com reader

The Way We Stay

A MEMOIR OF RECOVERY

CERE DEMUTH

The Way We Stay - A Memoir of Recovery

Second Edition

©2018 by Cere Demuth
All rights reserved.

Book design by W. Bruce Conway
Cover Illustration by Rebecca Caridad

ISBN 978-1-5323-8959-7

Printed by Ingram Spark
Distributed by Ingram Content Group

To Carter,
Canon, and Clementine;
the motivation for it all.

Where you go I'll go,
where you stay I'll stay.

—Ruth 1:16

I took my love, I took it down
I climbed a mountain and I turned around
And I saw my reflection in the snow-covered hills
'Til the landslide brought me down

—Stevie Nicks
Fleetwood Mac
"Landslide"

*For most people recovery means not having
to keep secrets from yourself, including
secrets about the ways you have
managed to survive.*

—Bessel van der Kolk

Preface

I began writing this book simply as an exercise. I committed to writing for thirty minutes a day for one year. I knew I had an abundance of thoughts, feelings, and memories that needed to be cleared out of my mind. I needed, finally, to lay it all down.

After about thirty days of writing, I realized I had a story to tell. Thus I began to tell the story of my son's addiction, and the story of our life together, which was tainted by addiction from the beginning.

There are many people and places that are a part of this story, and to preserve them a few names have been changed but most have not; a handful of you are literally in the book, most of you are here in spirit. All of you are important. A memoir is a slice, a thin sliver of one persons' experience, in this case mine. Much more happened than I could fully capture, but I am hopeful you will be able to digest the essence of my experience, as well as a bit of the universal experience of loving a child who struggles with addiction.

I have many hopes for this book; the first, that it will help professionals and families to understand the insidious and painful nature of addiction; second, it will help people feel less alone with whatever addiction afflicts their lives and third, it will give you faith and make *staying* through the hardest of times just a little bit easier. Finally, I hope it allows you to breathe, if only for a moment.

Before

The beginning of the unraveling of my life was like the unraveling of a hand-knit sweater. My mom always told me never to pull on a loose thread. So, when I saw that loose thread of my life, I tucked it back inside just as she had taught me. I hoped it would never be seen and it wouldn't snag on anything. The loose thread made me uneasy though, it scared me to know my sweater could unravel at any moment, maybe even without me knowing. Every time I saw that loose, broken thread of my life I felt anxious. I told myself it didn't matter, it was only one little thread; as long as I didn't pull, nothing bad would happen.

ONE
Summer 2011

Nate is shooting up heroin.
The OxyContin isn't enough.
It's too hard to find.
It's too expensive.
He's too fucked up.

Stacy tells me he is shooting up in the bathroom.
The boys sit in the living room.
She is at work.

She's skinnier than usual.
His addiction is eating her up, too.
I beg her to go to counseling.
She finally does.

I tell her to get him out of the house.
If she doesn't, I will call Child Protective Services.
Her counselor says the same thing.
She knows we will.

Nate goes fishing.
She and the boys come visit us on Lampard Road.
I call an old friend from Al-Anon.
I ask him to take her to a meeting.

I drop her off in front of the Presbyterian church.
It's Saturday morning.
He meets her there.

After the meeting he takes her to the farmers market.
He pays for her to get a chair massage.

He tells her she has to take care of herself.

She listens.
She tries to understand.

She is weak and exhausted.
I pick her up and bring her home.
She is slowly gaining clarity.

We go to the annual Fly-In at the airport.
There are games, planes, and food to eat.
It's full of families and flight enthusiasts.
It's super hot.
We are all dripping with sweat.

Stacy and I try not to think about Nate.
We try not to think about heroin.
We try not to think about how bad it really is.

But we do.
Finally, it's so bad we can't pretend.
Something has to change.

Stacy has to change.
Stacy has to protect her boys.
Stacy has to protect herself.

I say the Serenity Prayer.
I put Stacy and Nate in God's hands.
I pray for the next right thing to happen.

I breathe.

TWO

Spring 1985

I never imagined I would be terrified.

But I was.

I sat in the passenger seat of my mom's dented, brown Honda Accord wagon with the non-functioning gas gauge. She ran out of gas more than anyone I knew, but thankfully not today. We finally made it to the parking lot of the emergency room at Whidbey General Hospital.

I changed my mind.

I didn't want to have a baby.

I couldn't do it.

What if something went wrong?

What if I failed?

I didn't want to have a baby.

I wasn't getting out.

"You have to," she said.

"You can do it the easy way or the hard way, Cere."

"Either way, this baby is going to be born."

"It's happening."

"Okay," I said.

I took a deep breath.

I took another.

Okay, okay.

I'm ready.

I'll do it the easy way, I said to myself.

My mom walked around and opened my door. We walked into the hospital, down the long white hall to the maternity wing. I had one more moment of panic as they led me to the birthing room. Seeing the incubators in the hallway terrified me. Everything that was about to happen terrified me. My whole life was about to change.

I held my breath.

This baby was three-and-half weeks early, which meant I was high-risk. I was already high-risk being a teenage mom. But my pregnancy had been normal and I had felt amazing the whole time, minus a couple months of mild morning sickness.

I wanted, and needed, this baby more than anything.

I began to breathe.

THREE
Fall 2002

Nate is using meth. I want to curl up and die. Deep inside my soul, I feel a vibration. It's fear. Everything I have ever believed about life and myself as a mother is betraying me.

My son is betraying me.

I'm sitting at the cheap particle-board desk in the kitchen looking out through the lattice windows covered in clear heavy-duty plastic. This is how all the yurt windows are in our unconventional home. Vida is napping in her bed on the floor. I'm researching treatment programs for adolescent drug addiction.

I feel like someone has reached into my gut and yanked my son from my womb. I fight back tears from the pain. The rage is even deeper. I refuse to be in denial that this is happening. I know the dangers of denial. At the same time, I refuse to accept it. I know in every part of my being that I have to save his life, and I will.

I am desperate to find the perfect place. I am familiar with a local program called Sundown. It's the oldest local treatment program in the state. It's a twelve-step program, twenty-eight days. It's in Yakima.

Many teens and adults over the years have completed the program at Sundown. Some leave and continue with the twelve steps of AA or NA and stay sober, but even more go right back to using. I know that treatment is just that, treatment, not a cure. It's one step of many in the healing process of addiction.

I have to find the right place, the perfect place, for Nate's first step towards healing. I think about all the trips to Edmonds these last few months to see Nate's therapist whose name I can't remember and whose help did not appear to help.

I call my own therapist. I leave a message. He calls me

back within an hour. Don listens. Don knows me. He helps hold my pain. He's been doing this with extraordinary skill every other week in ninety-minute appointments for most of the last five years.

It's late now. Dark. Nate is not home. He probably won't come home. He rarely comes home at night any more. When he does come home at night he often seems happy and chatty. It confuses me.

It feels personal, even intimate. This is the meth. It makes people talkative. The next day he is always angry and agitated. Everything I say to him is wrong. He is mean. Everything he does and says makes me hate him, and myself. I obsess about what I have done wrong that would cause him to do this to himself and me.

I read and reread the websites listing the symptoms of meth addiction. Yes, he smells different. He smells tinny. His face is full of sores. His skin looks grey. He looks dirty, even when he's clean. He's angry. He's violent. He hates me most of the time. He is no longer warm. He is no longer kind.

People used to envy the closeness of our relationship, but now we are strangers. We used to move through life together with an openness and connectedness that had the quality of siblings. Yet, I'd always been clear that I was his mother. I never burdened him with my needs, at least not consciously. I protected him.

I was a single mom the first eight years of his life, not quite an adult when he was born. We grew up together. We moved through the world as a unit. I protected and cared for him. He was on the forefront of every decision I made. He was my physical, psychological, and moral compass.

I feel ripped off, like a waitress in a podunk diner. The same diner I have dreamed of running away to a million times. I'm that waitress, the one who saved every tip she ever made for sixteen years, only to find that someone has stolen her jar of money.

I thought I was a good mom, until now.

More than anything else in this world I wanted to be a good mom. My own mom always told me how much I loved and cared for my baby dolls. At eleven, I became the favorite babysitter amongst a local group of moms. Later, as a teenager, I would say I didn't know if I wanted to get married, but I definitely wanted to be a mom.

I was always a mom first.

Every choice I made from the moment I found out I was pregnant, two weeks after my seventeenth birthday, was motivated by my desire to be a good mom. Where I chose to live. Who I chose to date. The profession I chose. The friends I chose. The books I read. The food I ate. The walks I took. I thought about my impact on Nate and his perception of me in every step and breath I took.

Now, I can hardly breathe.

Late at night when he is chatty I feel close to him and hopeful that he isn't using. The rest of the time he is agitated, angry, preoccupied, and I know something is desperately wrong. He sleeps. He has no regard for school, rules, boundaries, or expectations. I try not to come undone. On the outside I appear relatively calm. On the inside I am screaming, crying, and imagining throwing up.

Driving through town I try to catch a glimpse of him. Is that him on the bench in front of Wells Fargo? Is he hanging out by the ferry terminal and the public lockers where I have heard drug dealers keep their drugs? I long to see him, as if somehow it will make him more okay than he actually is. He is never home when he says he will be, or when I ask him to be. I spend most of my time calling his friends or driving to their houses to see if he might be there. He rarely is.

His friends from childhood no longer associate with him. They look at me with blank stares. They don't know if I know how bad Nate is and they don't want to be the ones to tell me. I can see it in their eyes. Nate is as much a stranger to them as he is to me. I want to tell them, it's okay, I know. But I can't bear saying it.

I feel sick and angry all the time. The anger turns to rage. Underneath the rage is shame. I must be a bad person or this wouldn't be happening to me. There is also guilt. Maybe I shouldn't have sent him to that one summer camp? Did someone sexually abuse him? I shouldn't have adopted Vida. I shouldn't have had that one boyfriend. I never should have married Larry. All of this is my fault.

If it is my fault then maybe I can fix it.

I feel sick.

Again.

Alisha, a girl a few years older than Nate, answers the door. He is not there, again. The house smells weird like Fabreez and metal and cigarettes. I hate this smell. This is what meth smells like. I go home to look for him. I find pieces of burnt tinfoil on Nate's bedroom floor. I go in his room when he is not home and search for clues of what he is doing and why he is acting this way.

Why isn't he acting like my son?

Why is he doing this to himself?

Why is he doing this to me?

I ask myself a hundred times a day.

I pace in the yurt kitchen. Vida is toddling around. She is fifteen months old now. She is *muy contente*. This is what they used to say about her in Guatemala, and it is true.

I hate that this is the truth. I do my best to compartmentalize. It's the least I can do. I am not the same happy, hopeful mom that brought her home ten months ago. I feel like a horrible mom to both my children.

The phone rings.

Alisha has finally called.

"Alisha, is Nate using meth? Tell me the truth," I beg her.

"He is," she tells me.

"He's really messed up."

I know she's right.

But I needed to hear her say it, again.

I want to throw up. I imagine hanging my head over the toilet and puking out the contents of my stomach until I'm dry heaving.

Throwing up is how I used to try to feel some semblance of control. It started when I was fourteen and life was completely out of my control. The throwing up didn't last very long, as I wasn't very good at it. In my late twenties I discovered laxatives, which were much more discreet, easier, and still gave me a sense of control over my life when needed. Throwing up, though, is still my go-to fantasy when I am terrified.

I'm terrified.

I want to feel in control of my life again. I want some control over my son again. I want some influence, but I seem to have none. The desire to throw up consumes me.

I wade through the fantasy. I take a deep breath. I leave my mom-mode and go into therapist-mode. After ten years as a psychotherapist, I have practice with a certain degree of detachment. It's the only mode I am capable of functioning in given the situation. I am not sure this is a good thing, but I know it's better than throwing up or lying down on the wood floor in the middle of my kitchen in a fetal position.

I still have a toddler to care for, a practice and a home to manage. I have to keep myself together.

I breathe.

FOUR

August 1984

After that night with Glen I just knew I was pregnant. As the days and weeks progressed I was nauseous, tired, my breasts were tender, my period was late, and I couldn't stand the smell of nearly anything. I called Mr. Willis, my school counselor, and asked him about my credits. Did I have enough to graduate early?

I did.

I called my friend, Kären who was a nurse at the Langley Clinic and had been a mentor to me since I was fourteen and babysitting her daughter. Kären taught me the pleasures of Vantage cigarettes and glasses of red wine late into the night. She was tall, slender, and always poised. She was beautiful with her dark hair and olive complexion. Confident and honest, she pulled off an unshaven bikini line with grace. She was well read, sophisticated, and cultured.

I had watched Kären survive a painful divorce to one man and fall madly in love with another. She cared for Erin with intention, tenderness, and patience. She was everything my mother wasn't and I trusted her. She met me at the clinic and we waited in an exam room for the results of my pregnancy test.

It was positive.

I felt weak.

I cried.

Dr. Shapiro, who had been my doctor and family friend since I was a little girl, was kind and concerned. His long, curly, brown hair was tied back in a ponytail and his warm, steady way was calming. He told me, very seriously, *the good times will be as good as the bad times are bad.* I thought about what that meant over and over again.

I had to tell my mom. Maybe she already knew, because when I asked her to go on a walk she immediately made time for me. She listened calmly as we walked down Third Street past the Catholic church and under the deep-purple leaves of the flowering plums. Of course I knew inside she was sad and worried for me, but she remained neutral on the outside.

She didn't pass judgment on me. She made sure I knew my options and that I knew the difficulty of each one. Ultimately, she assured me she would support me no matter what I chose.

My mom told my dad, and he was disappointed in me. He was angry at me and my mom when he found out I wanted to stay pregnant. He blamed her.

He was embarrassed and vocal about his wish for me to have an abortion. I hated him for it. I felt betrayed and judged. He finally came around, but underlying his support I would feel his chronic disappointment in me as his daughter for years to come.

By the time I told Glen, he had already heard it through the grapevine. He suggested we get married. I said no. I couldn't be a mother *and* a wife. That was too much. He asked about abortion, but I was firm in my decision to keep this baby.

I pushed him away. We saw each other every day at school, passing in the halls in deafening silence. The heaviness between us was unbearable. My heart literally ached. Sometimes we avoided each other's eyes, other times we locked eyes longing for some better way. But we were in some kind of emotional molasses, unable to move any closer or any further from each other. We were stuck in fear. We were children pretending to be adults, completely unprepared.

When I was ten weeks pregnant I panicked. I drove over to his house and cried in his arms. I had changed my mind. I didn't want to have a baby. I asked him if he would help me pay for an abortion.

He said, "No. You will resent me for the rest of your life if you have an abortion. I don't have the money and I am not going to try and get it for you." The moment he said it, I relaxed. I committed fully to the baby inside me.

I was going to school in the mornings and working at the Children Center, the nonprofit childcare center my mom ran and directed, from one to six Monday through Friday. I craved bacon cheeseburgers and Campbell's tomato soup, anything salty.

My mom moved out of my dad's and rented an apartment on Sixth Street. She was ready to have her own place again, and I wanted to live with her, not my dad. We didn't see eye to eye on my pregnancy. He wasn't helpful or patient. My mom was both.

I lived with her until January when I rented my own place. It was a four-plex on Edgecliff Drive. I finished up my high school classes in January and graduated a semester early. My baby was due at the end of May.

I was relieved to be out of high school. I was content working and preparing my apartment for my baby. I sewed a few blankets, crib bunting, and curtains for the nursery. I hung paintings on the walls and decorated with mementos from my own unfinished childhood. I chopped firewood and kept the house warm using the woodstove. I missed Glen and wondered if I was doing the right thing. He missed me too, but we were too upset to talk.

My friends were sweet. Ursula, Cindy, and Raina came by occasionally and did their best to stay in touch. Our lives were so different. I was lonely, but also satisfied to have such a clear purpose for my life.

I visited my friend Tia in Everett. We stayed in touch in the summers since she moved. We had gone to the long-awaited summer dances, at Bayview Hall, with her cousin Suzanne, and spent many nights hanging out drinking vodka and smoking those Marlboro Lights. When I visited her it was fall and I was newly pregnant. I don't even think I had told her yet, and when I came downstairs, she had several lines of coke on the kitchen counter. It was the first time I had been around cocaine. She asked if I wanted some.

If it wasn't for the baby inside me I would have snorted that coke in a heartbeat. I wouldn't have cared what it would do to my body or my life. But, being pregnant changed that. I liked how my body felt. I liked knowing what was expected of me. I felt stronger and clearer about who I was while pregnant. I had a purpose.

As the months passed, I became more independent, and more pregnant. I read Dr. Spock and every pamphlet that the WIC nurse gave me.

I finished my last day of work on a Friday. I had one more month until my due date and I was planning to wash baby clothes and prepare all the last-minute things I would need. I was not in a rush.

I walked into Langley that Sunday to window shop and get some exercise. I had been walking every day. It was a crisp, clear spring day. I was browsing at Virginia's Antiques when all of sudden I felt a wetness between my legs, as if I'd peed myself. I asked Virginia if I could use her bathroom, where I realized my water had broken. My heart beat fast and hard.

I walked home. I called my mom and Dr. Shapiro. I wasn't really having contractions, so I waited at home to see if labor would begin on its own. My mom waited and walked with me as I had a few contractions, though still not too many and not too strong.

We went to dinner at La Casita for some spicy food, which I hoped would help bring on labor. Kate was playing her guitar and singing "Circle Game," one of my favorites. I ate chips and cheese, and lots of salsa, but my labor stayed slow and weak.

By morning there was still no real labor to speak of. My mom had been a birthing assistant since my brother was born at home. Throughout the years she had taken me to attend and help with at-home-births most of my life. Because of that, I trusted her instincts and her assessment of my labor. We called the Langley Clinic again; Dr. Shapiro was not on call, so Dr. Alderdice would deliver. Since my water broke and my labor was not progressing, I needed to be induced.

The idea of an IV terrified me more than giving birth. I had no choice. I took a shower and prepared to go to the hospital. Still dripping from the shower, I asked my mom to take a photo of my belly. My contractions were few and far between. I felt their ripple, but they weren't strong.

By the time I was in the hospital bed and hooked up to monitors it was three in the afternoon. My dad, my brother, and a few friends had arrived about the same time. Dr. Alderdice started the Pitocin drip and within an hour my contractions were coming full force. I could not talk between them and it took every bit of me to get through them.

My mom on my left, a friend of my mom's, Nadean, at my feet, and the nurse on my right. Everyone else was in the waiting room. With the beginning of each contraction I took a deep breath and made eye contact with my mom. As the contractions peaked I focused on Nadean, who rubbed my feet and worked pressure points to ease my pain and help my labor progress.

While I breathed I focused on the ceiling vent, which was a spiral, and I visualized my cervix was a spiral, opening. Weeks before I had seen a movie at the Clyde about a teenage girl surfer, so through each contraction I imagined I was riding a wave. I was on a surfboard finding just the right balance of holding on and letting go. Over and over again, I repeated the spiral pattern and surfing image until seven at night, when it was finally time to push.

Pushing was scary and embarrassing, but necessary. I was quiet. I was internal. I had to completely let go and trust my body. I had to allow it to open and let this baby out. I didn't want to, but I did. The baby's head was crowning.

I pushed, and I held back.

I breathed.

I pushed, and held back.

I breathed.

I pushed again.

And there he was.

Dr. Shapiro arrived at the last minute and caught him. He placed my sweet, slippery, baby boy into my arms. Warm tears of joy and relief streamed down my cheeks. My body was shaky and weak.

He was okay.

We were okay.

We were alive.

I called him Nate, which meant "gift from God." No matter what I did or did not believe about God, somehow I knew in my heart that's exactly what he was.

I breathed.

FIVE

Winter 2002

I know Alisha well. I remember when we met. It was 1990 and we were both at the Sunshine Laundromat on Nichols Street. She was hanging out by herself watching the laundry for her mom. She had big brown eyes, an olive complexion, and thick dark hair. She was a beautiful waif of a girl.

She was about seven years old. She was a bit disheveled, a little dirty, and very outgoing. She chatted away. She told me about her family—her mom, her dad, and her brother. She told me her mom was really young and she'd had her brother when she was fifteen years old. I told her I was seventeen when I had Nate, and from that moment on we were bonded. In the laundromat, I could see that Alisha had to take care of herself. She was charming, precocious, and quick as a whip.

Now, eleven years later, she and my son are hanging out. I think he is doing meth at her house. It doesn't make sense, and at the same time it does. She is two years older than him. She is overly familiar with the drug scene. She also has a huge heart. She is a giver. I don't know if she is using too, but I assume she is just on the periphery, enabling.

She knows I care about her. She knows how much I love Nate. She betrays Nate's trust because she knows I will take action. I love her even more for this.

No one wants to tell you when your child is on drugs. They either think you know or they think you are oblivious. Maybe they have empathy for you or maybe they think you deserve it and that it's your fault. Regardless, no one tells you.

Later, Alisha will tell me that Nate told her I would never send him away to one of those programs. Nate underestimates me because that's exactly what I'm about to do.

I know in every part of my being this is life or death. I have some money from my Auntie Barb; it is for Nate's college tuition. If he is dead he won't be going to college, so I rationalize that now is the time to spend the money.

I owe him that.

I frantically make calls the next morning. There are hundreds of programs; indoor, outdoor, on a ranch, military, lock down, two months, six months, one year, four years. If you have the money there are so many places to send your addicted, angry, mentally ill, noncompliant child. I do not want to be in this club.

Finally my brother finds a place that doesn't seem too awful; it's called Anasazi. They seem to understand that my son is not *that* sick, *that* addicted, or *that* crazy.

Anasazi was started by Mormons and has both a spiritual and survivalist approach. The program believes that in order for a child to heal they must change their hearts. They believe parents' hearts must change, too. They teach that one can't effect change in their child without healing their own hearts. When our hearts and our children's hearts heal, the relationship will change, and healthy, safe behaviors will follow. The way they talk about children and change in their mission statement speaks to me:

> "At ANASAZI, the children come first, and adults come second. To free themselves from worldly cares, attendees are advised to 'drop their burdens at the gate' and tend to the needs of the YoungWalkers on the trail. We strive to remind ourselves that the ANASAZI way is not to change the behavior of the YoungWalker or the parents, but to provide opportunities for the heart to be touched, so the change can come willingly from the 'one who stands within.' Then the change of heart, like clear water, will flow without compulsion."
>
> —*The One Who Stands Within* by
> Good Buffalo Eagle, Ezekiel C. Sanchez

I agree with this approach in theory. Although, I am also still in denial about how bad Nate's addiction is. I am in denial about how angry and closed off he is to me. But I am hopeful that we will all heal. I am hopeful that Nate will stop using meth after going to this program. I am hopeful this will at least keep him alive.

They have a space for Nate, tomorrow.

I call my friend June and ask her to come over. June does not hesitate. She is my confidant, my closest friend, and she knows the details of my terror. We felt an immediate connection when we met as young mothers on the ferry ten years ago.

I call my husband, Larry, at work and tell him we are taking Nate to treatment in Arizona and we will be leaving tonight to go to Whidbey Island. We will stay at my dad's tonight in Langley and be on a plane to Arizona tomorrow morning. I call my mom, my dad, and my brother. I deliver to each of them the bad news. I hear the sadness, pain, fear, and worst of all the judgment and doubt in their voices. I ask for their help anyway.

I need help.

I am already exhausted. I am orchestrating an emergency rescue. My fear for Nate's life and my adrenaline keeps me going. I am more than familiar with emergencies.

Up until recently I have been on call one week a month for San Juan County's mental health emergencies. I answered calls and showed up at the medical center, the jail, and even at people's homes to assess their suicide risk. At times, I flew in a small airplane with them to mental health hospitals off-island.

I have yet to tell Nate about this particular emergency, which is his life. I expect him to be home soon. I wait for him and for June. I need June to be with Vida while I explain the plan to Nate.

June is not surprised to get my call.

She does not hesitate.

She comes right away.

We wait for Nate.

June and I have been especially close through Vida's adoption and the decision-making leading up to it. Having been abandoned by her own birthmother as a newborn, and later adopted, she has developed a special bond with Vida. She is my favorite person to smoke a Marlboro Light with— although it's very rare, and Larry vehemently disapproves.

When Nate arrives home I will have to tell him I know about his meth use and I am sending him to an outdoor treatment program for six to eight weeks. My heart is beating uncharacteristically fast.

I am terrified he won't comply.

I am terrified of losing him. I am terrified he will die. My body feels hot. I am on high alert. I am listening and listening and listening for Nate to drive up the driveway.

I set June and Vida up in her bedroom with toys, books, and a snack. There is a little wooden slide in Vida's room and a mattress for her bed on the floor. Her dresser, which was mine as a girl, and Nate's when he was little, is now painted orange, pink, and purple.

These are the colors of all her things, including the cut-velvet quilt I made while waiting to pick Vida up in Guatemala. It's full of deep purples violet, and orange scraps. The blanket my mother knit Vida with the popcorn stitch she is famous for lays folded on her bed. Strands of orange, purple, and hot pink alternating in a three-by-four soft wool blanket, just for Vida. She also knit her a hooded cardigan sweater that matches.

Nate has a blanket and matching hooded cardigan my mom knit almost seventeen years ago. The colors are a muted blue, lavender, white, and mint green. She knit the same little sweater for me when I was a baby, only it was dark green. The blanket and sweater are in a special box of keepsakes, which he can one day share with his babies. These days, I wonder if he will even live to have babies.

Waiting.

Listening.

Rapid heartbeats.

Long, slow, deep breaths.

At last, Nate is home. He walks right into his room. I follow him.

"Nate, I have to talk to you." My heart is beating fast. Nate is nearly six feet tall and weighs 185 pounds. He is only sixteen and a half, but he is a big man. I am frightened he will hurt me. Just last week when he was angry at me, he punched his fist into the front window of my car while I was driving him home from town.

He can feel my tension. I know he has seen June's car in the driveway. He asks me where Vida is and I tell him she's with June in her room. This is rare. Everything feels different to me and, I suspect, to him. I am scared, but outwardly calm.

"Nate," I say, "I know you are using meth."

"I am not!" he yells.

"Nate, I know you are."

"You stay up all night."

"You are losing weight."

"You are angry and agitated."

"Or, you are overly happy and talking a lot."

"I AM NOT USING METH!" he yells at me.

"You are," I say.

"I want you to go to treatment."

"There is an outdoor treatment program in Arizona."

"It's called Anasazi."

"Oliver found it."

"I AM NOT GOING!"

"YOU'RE CRAZY!"

"I FUCKING HATE YOU!"

"I AM NOT FUCKING GOING!" he screams.

"Yes," I tell him.
"You are."

He wants to leave. I stand in his way. I block his doorway. Nate tries to get past me. He physically pushes me out of his way. My voice is getting louder and more powerful, but still calm and metered.

"You have to go."
"I won't let you leave here until you agree."
"You are going to kill yourself if you keep using."
"I want you to be safe."
"I don't want you to use meth."
"I don't want you to die."

I feel his body pushing me and wanting to fight me. I know I have to stay strong.

"We are taking the four o'clock ferry.

We are driving down to Whidbey and we will spend the night with Papa Skip. Grammy will come with us to take care of Vida. In the morning we will drive to Sea-Tac and get on a plane to Phoenix. Someone from Anasazi will meet us there and you will go with them and start on your journey. You will be gone six to eight weeks."

"NO!"
"I HATE YOU."
"I FUCKING HATE YOU!" he screams again.

He's scared.
I see it in his eyes.

"I know you hate me, Nate."
"I'm sorry."
"This is all I know to do."

Larry, Grammy, Vida, and I will stay at a hotel. Larry and I will participate in a parenting program for two days while

25

my mom watches Vida. We have to learn new skills, too. It's not Nate's fault. We all have to change. Addiction is a family disease.

I tell him again, "I am sorry, Nate."
"This isn't what I wanted for you, for us."
"I love you."
I'm beginning to cry.
But I stop myself.

"I AM NOT GOING TO SOME FUCKING OUTDOOR TREATMENT PROGRAM!"

"I know you are scared," I offer.
"What you are doing is not working."
"It is not okay."
"You are not okay."
His face is red. He is banging the wall and moving his things around loudly. He moves his big body towards me. He wants to leave. I fear that he will hurt me. I tell him he is scaring me. My heart is beating hard and fast.
"If you don't calm down I will call the police."
"If you hurt me I will press charges," I say.
"I will tell them you are using meth."
"I will give them all the names of your friends who are using meth."
"You can follow my plan, calm down, and start packing, or I can call the police."
We are still in the doorway between his yurt bedroom and the kitchen. June and Vida are still in Vida's room. He takes a deep breath. He is very agitated, gritting his teeth and clenching his jaw, but he backs away from me. I can see he doesn't really want to hurt me. He also does not want me to call the police.
"Would it be easier if you could bring a friend with us?" I ask.

"Yes," he says.

"How about Alisha?"

He agrees. I call Alisha as we stand there, still in the hall-way between his bedroom and the kitchen. I am still blocking him from leaving. Alisha answers. I tell her what I have just told Nate. I ask her, or rather beg her, to come with us. We will be leaving in about an hour. Can she come help Nate? She says yes. I tell Nate, even though he can hear the conversation. He relaxes a bit more.

I relax a bit, too. We have a plan. I call Larry at work, my dad, and my mom and tell them the plan is in place. I call Anasazi to confirm that we will be there tomorrow afternoon. I hate that this is happening. I hate that this is my life.

I feel sick.

I go into Vida's bedroom and tell June. Vida and June are playing, but I know they have been scared. June tells me later that the yelling was scary. She has protected Vida as best as she can. She is calm for me.

I have to pack. I pack the cutest dresses for Vida. I talk with her. I stay close to her as we get ready. It feels surreal. I think, this can't be my life. I don't even believe in sending children away. I believe in staying and working things out. But we can't work anything out. He is almost seventeen years old and addicted to meth.

I am a therapist in a small town and my son is a meth addict.

How in the hell did I get here?

What have I done wrong?

Is what I'm doing going to help?

Or is it going to make him worse?

I don't know.

But it's all I know to do.

Adrenaline is moving through my body. June has gone

home. Alisha is at the house. Larry is home, too. We are almost packed. We load our luggage into the dark blue Toyota Previa. It's the minivan I bought to drive my teenage son and his friends to football and baseball games. Instead I am driving my family to the airport to go to a drug treatment program. This is not the life I imagined for myself, my son, or my daughter.

I feel sick.

Again.

I cancel the rest of my clients for the week. I call Anne and tell her Vida won't need childcare for the rest of the week. I call Don and leave him a message telling him what I am doing. I call Nate's therapist, cancel his next appointment. I am furious with him because he has been useless.

I am enraged that all my hard work as a mom has not paid off. Everything I have worked for since Nate's conception has turned to shit.

We drive down to the ferry and wait. I am glad Alisha is with us, and she keeps Nate calm. We finally load and endure the long, slow ferry ride, then drive down Whidbey to my dad's. Tomorrow morning we will fly to Arizona.

My beautiful baby girl rests on my lap. She is innocent, sensitive, smart, strong, a miracle in my life. I want to give her everything and Nate is taking that away. At the same time he is also taking away everything I gave him.

I can barely breathe, but I do.

SIX
Winter 2000

Larry let me adopt Vida. It wasn't something he had actually wanted for himself, but he gave into my longing to be a mother again. Larry gives in to me more than he should. More than is healthy.

He was unwilling to do artificial insemination, but willing to adopt. I really wanted to be pregnant again. I loved being pregnant with Nate and I knew I would enjoy it even more now that I was an adult.

Larry feels there are already too many children in the world. If we can't reverse his vasectomy with the confidence of getting pregnant naturally, he thinks we should adopt. We have consulted a specialist in Seattle about vasectomy reversal who says there is a very low percentage of it being successful for someone his age. I am afraid of adoption.

I have mixed feelings about adoption.

When I was pregnant with Nate, my neighbor had spotted me walking across First Street in Langley. She yelled my name, "Cere, Cere…" I stopped and she came over to tell me that she had a friend who really wanted to adopt a baby, and maybe she could adopt mine. I was over six months pregnant and completely attached to this life inside me. It felt like someone was trying to rip my baby from my arms. How could couples just take another woman's baby?

But, if I want to be a mom again and to do it within my marriage, my only option is adoption. I lament. I meditate. I dream about it. I watch Oprah on Monday afternoons at three. I wonder what I might do with the rest of my life if I do not have another child. Even though I love my work, it is simply not enough.

My whole adult life I have had a child to care for. I can't imagine my life, as a woman in my thirties, without a small child. I do not want to read a book on the ferry back and forth to the mainland. I want to take care of a child on the ferry, play UNO, color, eat fries, drink hot chocolate. I am not done being a mom.

Nate is almost fifteen. He has three more years of high school. I am nine years into my career, living on a small island in a small town, and married to someone twenty-five years my senior.

What the fuck am I doing?

A part of me wants to leave. I want to move to Seattle with Nate where he can attend a better school and I can challenge myself professionally. My consultant, my psychotherapist, a vibrant psychoanalytic community, live music, great food, and interesting people are all in Seattle.

But I am married. I made a commitment to Larry, to his family, to Nate. I have created stability for myself and Nate. I have a beautiful life, a beautiful view, a long and beautiful dirt road to drive home on every night. Why would I change any of that? Instead of leaving the world I have created with Larry, I could share all of this with a new life, a new daughter. I would be a grown-up mom, instead of a teenage mom. I am afraid to stay and I am afraid to go. I watch more Oprah on Monday afternoons. I contemplate my choices.

What do I want most?

To be a mom again or to have the freedom and independence of a single adult life? Do I want to keep this little island life as a mother of a teenager, wife of an older man, and simply be a small-town psychotherapist? Or do I want to run away with my son to the city and risk the exposure of more dangers to Nate? I would have to work more hours building a city practice that could support him and me.

What if I failed?

What if Nate got in with the wrong crowd?

What if the disruption and loss were too much for him?

What if he hated me for it?

What if he started using drugs?

Am I more afraid to leave or to stay? Staying has always been my mantra. Staying has felt like my life's work. Wayne Dyer is on Oprah one afternoon. He is talking about making decisions and suggests asking yourself, "If you weren't afraid, what would you do?" In that one moment I know my answer. If I wasn't afraid I would adopt a baby girl from Guatemala.

I have already researched the different types of adoption, all the countries, all the risks and benefits of each option. Guatemala has the most well-cared-for, youngest, and healthiest babies. Because of my work I am aware enough to have concerns about attachment, bonding, addiction issues, and general infant mental health.

Guatemala does not have the addiction issues we have here in the States with domestic adoption. The main reasons for adoption in Guatemala are poverty, sexual abuse, and the strict rules of Catholicism. Their foster care system is stable. Infants are typically not placed in orphanages.

I decide. Larry and I decide. We are going to adopt a baby girl from Guatemala. I choose an agency and start the arduous process of gathering documents and completing the onslaught of paperwork required for a Guatemalan adoption.

As soon as we make our decision I tell Nate. I want him to have time to prepare emotionally. As we sit on the bed in his little yurt bedroom, the baseball field mural is still vibrant above us from the bottom bunk. "We are going to adopt a baby girl from Guatemala. I have thought about it for a long time, over a year, and I love being your mom so much I want to be a mom again. I am not done."

He stays neutral, standoffish, maybe a little curious about this baby sister that will be joining us in the next year, but he is definitely not happy. I assure him about how much I love him and that I will still be here for him. I see in his bright blue eyes that he doesn't believe me. I also feel it in my gut, he feels betrayed by me, more than betrayed, deeply wounded. I push that feeling down. I tuck that thread in because I can't bear the thought of losing him, or not being a mother again. Instead I focus on his words. "Okay, Mom," he says. "If that's what you want." I ignore the confused look on his face. I tell myself he's not quite fifteen, he can't really imagine what having a baby sister will feel like. I tell myself he will be okay.

We will be okay.

In the spring of Nate's freshman year, he tries out for high school baseball. He has a girlfriend, Julia. He is getting good grades and is home for dinner every night. He brings Julia and Adrian on a trip to Cannon Beach. I take photos on the vast ocean beach, and Haystack Rock. We drive down and visit the campground I took Nate to when he was two.

By the time I was fifteen I was already lost. I was having sex, drinking, taking uppers, and rarely coming home. I was disconnected from my parents and school. I was working two jobs, hanging out with friends late into the night, and preparing to move out of my father's house for the first time. Nate, and his life, is so different than mine. He is already fifteen and none of these things are happening. He has escaped the dangers of adolescence.

I am naive.

Spring is full of excitement. We are going to high school baseball games. Nate is a freshman so he doesn't play much, but they have a great team, a winning pitcher, and excellent coaches. We go to all the on-island games at Hartman Field and many off-island games. Sitting in the sun watching baseball, I am so proud of him. I can't believe how good he is, and how good our life is.

I have been taking photos and I am learning how to print and process film on my own. I spent one quarter taking a class at the Photography Center Northwest in Seattle. For the first time in my life, I have the time and opportunity to learn an art. I set up a darkroom in my office kitchen. I bring my telephoto lens attached to Larry's 1970s Pentax everywhere.

I take photos of Nate and his friends at Eagle Cove playing bocce ball, skimboarding, and goofing off. I have hundreds of baseball and football photos as well. I have a personal project photographing teenage mothers. This consumes me for hours when Nate is at school, or practice, or with Julia.

I have never been happier, except, I know there is something missing in my marriage. I hope I can tolerate it. I ignore it and tuck it away. I tell myself not to tug at that thread. So much good surrounds me. I do my best to focus on the good.

Before the summer is over, I have gathered piles of adoption paperwork and we are waiting for news of a baby girl in Guatemala. Larry's oldest, Heather, is married in the peak of the summer at the home of her husband-to-be on Bainbridge Island. I cook, with June's help, take photos, and give the step-mother role my whole heart. We tell her and her two younger brothers, who are all in their twenties now, about our adoption plans. Larry had wanted to wait until after the wedding. His sons are excited, but it is not easy for Heather. Larry does his best to soothe her. I feel horrible, but she cannot accept comfort from me and I am unwilling to change our plans.

Larry works in the garden the rest of the summer, supports me in the adoption, and agonizes over Heather's grief. I see clients three days a week and prepare for our baby. Nate works at Kings Market and hangs out with his friends and Julia, and starts football in the fall.

But soon Nate starts to come home smelling of pot, and I hear him talking more about alcohol and drugs. I wonder if it's because of our decision to adopt.

The only thing I know to do is to keep Nate close to home. I have bouts of fear. I don't trust him, myself, or the adolescent world. As a teenager myself, I took major risks with drugs, alcohol, and sex. Nate has always been that child, although good-natured and typically happy, who pushed the boundaries. Whatever boundary it was, he had to see what would happen if he stepped over the line. It was, and is, exhausting.

Even more alarming, as a psychotherapist in this small town, I know too much about what drugs are being used, which teens are using, and where they are using them. I know more about the nightlife of teens than the average parent; and it deeply affects my parenting. I wish I could be just slightly naive, like so many of the parents I know who are unaware of what their teens are actually up to late in the night. Before I know it, I am parenting out of fear.

I am holding on.

Very tight.

Too tight.

Since our decision to adopt, Nate seems more distant and more interested in things I don't approve of or value. He is testing my limits more. Eminem is rapping his angry and vile lyrics on the radio, the movies he watches are more vulgar and inappropriate than when I was his age. I am trying and failing at setting boundaries. He begins listening to hip-hop and watching gangster-themed movies. I turn off the movies, I talk about the movies. I turn off the music, I talk about the music. I am not really protecting him. I don't know how. I do not understand the power or influence this media is having on his life. It is eroding Nate's healthiest self and building up his anger and tolerance for life with drugs, sex, alcohol, and vile language. It's normalizing risky behavior and Nate is susceptible.

A nervousness is growing deep in my belly.

Have I made the right choice to adopt?

Is Nate going to be okay?

Isn't it normal to feel some disconnection?

Isn't this what healthy separation feels like?

I am waiting; waiting for news of our adoption.

The agency we have chosen tells us that adoptions are moving slow in Guatemala. Something doesn't feel right so I begin to investigate using an adoption facilitator I have heard about named Rusty, instead of the agency.

In mid-October I have a series of dreams. On the nights of October fifteenth, sixteenth, and seventeenth I dream about a baby. In one dream a baby is in a car seat, alone in the bleachers at a football game. No one is around and it is clear this baby was left for me to care for. When I realize no one is coming for the baby, I am uneasy. I sit with the baby. Finally, I take her home.

The second night, I dream that I am waiting for the ferry. I am standing on the dock and a dark haired, brown-skinned woman hands me her baby in a car seat and asks me to take care of her. She leaves on the ferry. I try to stop her. She won't stop. I stay and take care of her baby.

On the third night, I have the final dream. There is another baby abandoned in a car seat and needing a mother.

Again, I am the only one there and I take the motherless baby in my arms. I wake up on October eighteenth and call Rusty. I ask him if he would facilitate our adoption. He says yes. I feel like I am making the right decision. My body relaxes.

I fax Rusty all our paperwork. I call the other agency, inform them of our decision, and forfeit our deposit. Larry is not too happy, however he continues with his usual support. I am confident that Rusty will be able to unite us with the baby girl who is meant to be ours.

On November second, we receive an email from Rusty saying he wants to talk with both of us. I call Larry at school and he comes home early so we can receive Rusty's call together. We gather around the office desk in the back yurt and Rusty calls. The phone is on speaker so we can both hear him say a little girl has been born on October eighteenth, the night of my last dream. She weighs seven pounds, six ounces and is twenty-one inches long. Her name is Luisa Fernanda Cruz. She has been given the same name as her fifteen-year-old mother.

He emails us a Polaroid photo of her dressed in a fancy

white dress with pink embroidered trim. Her little hands are curled up by her chin. The photo makes me a little uneasy. She doesn't look like any baby I have ever seen. She is dark skinned and has a full head of spiky black hair. She is beautiful, but something about the way her hands are curled up makes me think something is wrong. I gather as much information from Rusty as I can.

Baby Luisa has been in a foster home since she was two days old. She is reportedly healthy and available for adoption. Her birth mom is too young to care for her.

She is the oldest of nine children in a single-parent home. Their family cannot feed one more mouth. We agree we want to adopt her, but before the final decision is made I want to go to Guatemala and meet her. I fly alone to Guatemala on Thanksgiving Day.

I stay for five days.

She is healthy, alert, strong, and well cared for by her foster mom. I feel better meeting the family who is caring for her. I am able to leave her with the blanket I have sewn and I am becoming acquainted with her country. We have to wait for paperwork to move through the legal system. It is the nature of Guatemalan adoption to go slow.

It is the nature of everything in Guatemala to go slow.

Vida Luisa is the name we choose for our baby girl. Luisa, since this is her given name and her birth-mother's name, and Vida because Nate chose it.

It means "life," and I loved that it's Nate's idea. Nate informs me that Vida is also a female rapper and he plays her popular song for me, which is basically her singing Vida, Vida, Vida in a long, beautiful melody.

Nate loves it. I love that he names her because it means he is becoming more invested and attached to this sister he has yet to meet and has been so ambivalent about. Larry does not object, although he is not thrilled.

Leaving Vida in Guatemala is excruciating. I return to Friday Harbor with rolls of film to develop and a hole in my arms where I held and slept with my daughter for five dream-like days. I have a small Beanie Baby with black hair, brown skin, and wearing a red sundress. I carry this doll with me wherever I go the next three-and-half months. I can still feel the humid Guatemalan heat and see the vibrant pink and purple bougainvillea climbing the walls outside my rented room.

I come home and prepare our family for a long planned trip to the Dominican Republic. Larry, Nate, and I will visit Nathan, Larry's oldest son. He is twenty-four and in the Peace Corps in a small mountain village of the Dominican Republic. We begin with a week at an all-inclusive resort in Punta Canta.

At the market in Punta Canta is a tattoo artist and Nate begs me to allow him to get one. There is no age restriction here. He wants a sun tattoo on his upper back. He has been wanting one, but in the States he has to wait until he is eighteen, so I acquiesce. I wonder if it is a bad or good decision. Larry shakes his head in disapproval, as he often doesn't agree with my parenting decisions. But I want to support Nate in anything that I don't consider ultimately harmful and as usual, I ignore Larry's disapproval. I know Nate is in a hurry to grow up and I am trying to hold him back and let him go at the same time.

The tattoo feels like a safe compromise.

After the tattoo and a week at the resort we ride in the back of small pickup truck to the top of a mountain, where we stay in Nathan's Peace Corps village. The little houses in the village have dirt floors and no running water. We stay for one week.

It is hot in Nathan's village. We rest in the shade. Nate reads a book in a hammock. We eat new foods and practice our Spanish. We play games with the children and attempt conversation in Spanish with the parents. We drink coffee with lots of sugar at every little house we visit.

The children love Nate, especially the little girls. One deaf and mute girl in particular attaches to him. I think her name is Elena. He is kind, gentle, and patient with her. I use rolls and rolls of film to document the people and the place. I use only black-and-white film and my telephoto lens. My favorite photo is one with Nate and the children climbing on his back and hanging on his arms.

My heart is open to the people, the place, and my family. I feel like I am six months pregnant as I think of Vida each day we are there. Everywhere I look I fall in love with the beauty of the place, the people, and the culture. I have my growing son, my supportive husband, and a fulfilled life for which I am grateful.

I don't think my life is perfect, but those little imperfections and things that don't feel right I hide away. Mainly it's the emotional distance between Larry and me that worries me. I comfort myself by imagining it is just a part of marriage, a part that will easily pass if I am patient. Although, I fear it will only widen. It's the loose thread of doubt, doubt about the health of my marriage, that I tuck deep inside so that even I can't see it.

I have already notified my clients that I will be taking a three-month leave of absence beginning in March. I know some of my clients may never come back, which saddens me, but it's unavoidable. I work carefully with each of my clients to prepare them for our separation.

My work is psychodynamic, which means I use the client-therapist relationship as a tool for understanding the connection between the present and the past. I focus on attachment and the need for some feelings of dependency on the therapist in order to heal the deeper attachment-related issues. This allows my clients to become more independent in a healthy way. My work is usually long term, so many of my clients have worked with me for one to several years. My practice consists of children, teens, and adults. Almost all my clients have experienced some form of trauma or abandonment.

And now, I will be taking care of someone else. I will be

giving someone else my full attention. I will be leaving my clients. But, I will also be coming back, I remind myself.

As I wait for Rusty to tell us Vida is legally free, I become increasingly concerned at how long it is taking. I research, in-depth, the best times for babies to separate from one attachment figure and attach to another. The research I find suggests around four to five months is a good time developmentally for that transition.

Given my research, instincts, and the potential timing of Vida's legal status, I decide to fly to Guatemala when she is five months old. March 17, 2001, the day before her five-month birthday, I will fly down and stay until the adoption paperwork is complete. I will live and care for her, while beginning the attachment and bonding process in Guatemala. She can adjust to me while still living with familiar smells, sounds, language, and weather.

The moon is full and orange as it sets over Guatemala City. It's five-thirty in the morning and the sky is a deep purple with a touch of pink and orange. The stars are still sparkling in the light of dawn. I gaze out the airplane window at the huge, orange, full moon as we prepare to land. Although I haven't grown this baby in my belly, I have been waiting exactly nine months since beginning this adoption process. Vida's birth is now imminent. I have butterflies in my stomach as the plane lands safely.

I breathe.

Vida is not quite six months old when, after a month with her in Guatemala, I finally board the plane to bring her home. My friend Suzi, also adopting, is on the same flight. Larry and Nate are at the airport to welcome us. Instead of driving home, Larry has chartered a flight to take us back to Friday Harbor.

I am flooded with mixed emotions. Larry is eager and overwhelms me with his emotions. I feel my walls go up as he comes toward Vida and me with his open arms, in them a beautiful quilt his coworkers made for Vida. I avert my eyes from his and focus on Vida and Nate. I can't let Larry in. I don't quite understand why and I don't try. I just tuck that loose thread inside and hope it doesn't unravel.

I am happiest and most relieved to see Nate. His smile means everything to me, and his open arms give me hope that he, we, will be okay. Vida is snuggled in close to my warm, tired, and finally relaxed, body.

The sky is all the shades of pink and orange as we fly north above Whidbey, over the Straits of Juan de Fuca and the San Juan Islands. Vida sleeps in my arms, eyes slightly open. Below we see Lopez Island, Cattlepoint, South Beach, Eagle Cove, and finally our tiny, Friday Harbor Airport.

Our landing is smooth. I have brought my daughter home safely all the way from Guatemala in one long day. With Vida in my arms, and tears in my eyes, I lean into Nate as we walk off the tarmac.

I have both my babies.

We live at the end of the road. The magic of this spot never escapes me. When the sun is out, it shines in our windows from morning till night.

San Juan Valley, False Bay, and the Olympics are spread out before us. Shore Pines line the property, and Ocean Spray and Queen Anne's Lace are scattered throughout. I've been taking in this view since shortly after my twenty-sixth birthday.

We live in a yurt, actually four yurts, up past the baseball field and the green water tower, at the end of Lampard Road. The road is lined with the small pink buds of the Nootka rose, wild blackberry bushes, and surrounded by Sundstrom's cow pastures, hay fields, and ponds. As I drive home, there are only a few houses spread out in five-acre parcels. The road is narrow. There is no center line and two cars can barely pass.

I've been walking up and down Lampard Road more than usual the last nine months since we adopted Vida. There is no place I would rather be than Lampard Road with Vida.

She spends most of her first year with me in the black, ring sling, which was woven and dyed in Guatemala. I strap her snuggly to my body. She is happiest there and I know it is important for our bond to recreate, as much as possible, that time in her birth-mother's womb. Wearing her is the best way to sync our bodies, smells, and heartbeats.

She grew in her mother's womb for nine months. She was in a foster home for five months. The first fourteen months of her life she was in sync or out of sync with two other mothers. She had attuned to them, not me. Now is the time for me to attune to her needs and feelings. It is our time to know each other's bodies, breath, and souls. I never pass her around at baseball games. I don't even let my own mother come meet her for a few weeks after I brought her home from Guatemala.

I don't let Larry feed her or take care of her basic needs. I wake up at night to comfort her. I feed Vida her bottle in the rocking chair every time. I respond to each and every one of her needs. For me this feels necessary and right. For Larry, this is difficult. With his first three children he was often the one to get up at night and his wife had welcomed any and all help. Since his first three were spaced so close together, all in a matter of five years, it was very different.

It is essentially effortless for me to care for Vida, perhaps because I have been a mom for so many years or because I had been single and so young the first time. I don't really feel like I need help. I savor every moment. I know it will go by too quickly. I know she will be my last.

However, I do still have to go back to work, and it comes too soon. In a perfect world I wouldn't go, but that's not part of my agreement with Larry. I resent that he's not willing to provide everything for me, for us. I resent that no one ever has. It's another one of those loose threads and as usual, I tuck it back in.

I find Anne, the very best person to care for Vida, and I return ten hours a week to my clients.

I breathe.

SEVEN

1986

By the time Nate was six months old, Glen was commercial fishing in Alaska and I was covered in baby spit-up. Being a mom was hard. Nate was colicky and I spent countless hours walking him, rocking him, and driving him around in the middle of the night.

It wasn't all colic. We had sweet times. I kept him close to me and loved nursing him, dressing him, singing to him, playing with him, and reading books to him.

The thirty-something moms in town welcomed me into their baby group. Every Friday we met at someone's house. They supported me when I told them I wanted to go to college. I loved waitressing and my mom was happy to watch Nate a few nights a week, but I knew I didn't want to be trapped as a waitress my entire life.

I had my transcripts sent to the Evergreen State College in Olympia. I called Evergreen and had them send me an application. By Thanksgiving I had been accepted.

I applied for financial aid and scholarships. By June, Nate and I were settled in Olympia, just a block from campus. My mom helped a little with money and she also took one day a week off work and drove to Olympia to watch Nate, which meant less time at the childcare center. My dad occasionally helped with a bit of cash, too.

Nate was barely one.

It wasn't easy. I was lonely and depressed.

Being nineteen years old, away from my hometown for the first time, a full-time student and single mother, I felt like I was waiting on the steps of a high dive, terrified. I set my life, our life, in motion and there was no turning back, no matter how excruciating, no matter the struggle. I had to climb the ladder, I had to dive in, every day.

I was a pretty good mom, but I made a lot of mistakes, too. I thought a lot about how to be a good parent. I wanted to be better than my parents in so many ways, but just as good in others. I wanted to be honest and real. I wanted to be kind, playful, and magical, like my mom. I did pretty well with that, except for when I was harsh and impatient, like my dad, which was usually when I was exhausted and Nate was loud or when he would not stop moving.

I had yet to learn how to regulate my own emotions, so I would yell, "Nate!!! Knock it off!" or grab his arm to get him to stop or come with me.

A handful of times I even spanked him, which made us both feel awful. Whatever the case may have been, I was impulsive at times. Like all children, Nate thrived on patience and I had a short fuse, which didn't serve him, and I imagine, left him at times feeling scared, hurt, not good enough, and angry at me. I did my best.

But I didn't understand the big energy of this boy of mine. He needed so much more than I realized or could ever have imagined. He pushed the limits. He wanted more from me; more back rubs at bedtime, more boundaries, more love, more time; more, more, more. I had no idea when I was pregnant he might need more than one seventeen-year-old girl could give him. It broke my heart, and his, that I was falling short. I was failing, but I was present. I wasn't on drugs. I barely drank. I didn't go to parties or spend hours hanging out with friends.

I had single-momma friends, too. We shared in the struggles and joys of being single moms who were working and going to school. One spring we hiked and camped at Mount Rainier with our babies and toddlers.

I borrowed their camping gear when Nate was two and took my first road trip. We went to the magical and protected Oswald Sands Beach on the Oregon Coast. The rain poured down on us the first night and we found a friend of a friend in Cannon Beach that let us hang out until we were dry and could try again the next night. It was the summer Nate potty trained and I was really starting to feel my power as an adult woman.

Although I felt powerful, sometimes I was simply exhausted and wanted to run away. I thought every day about my mom leaving me when I was two years old. Sometimes I fantasized about giving up, running away, leaving Nate, and driving east until I found a funky podunk diner in the Midwest. I imagined being a waitress in that funky podunk diner and renting a little rundown apartment above it. No one would know me and I would live a sad and lonely life, wishing I had never left, but comforted by the fact that I had no responsibilities.

I graduated from Evergreen in three years. It was a hot, sunny day when I walked across the stage in my green gown and hat, freckles out, and Nate on my hip, his bare feet hanging down past my thigh. My parents, with whom I had close, but often volatile relationships with, both came. They were so proud. My brother, my Auntie Barb, and my Grandma Natalie all came, too. We went to dinner that night to celebrate at the place I had been waitressing, Gardener's.

Nate and I moved back to Whidbey to get my bearings and apply to graduate school. I was quickly accepted to Antioch University in Seattle.

I wanted to help people. I had always been empathic and intuitive. Being raised at such a radical time in history and in my parents' lives made me more aware of widespread human suffering.

I knew a good therapist could make a difference. I wanted everyone who needed therapy to have that opportunity. I wanted to be that person for people. I wanted to be the person who stayed.

Being a therapist would make me a better mother, if I let

it. Being a therapist meant working on myself because I knew I could only help others to the extent that I could help myself. Antioch's master's program would take me two years.

I rented a little cabin on Whidbey near Scatchet Head. The cabin had a big covered porch looking out over a field, and on the edge of it was an alder forest. Rustic wood floors covered the cabin and the potbelly woodstove was in the center of the living room.

Nate and I ate at the counter. I made a lot of quesadillas in that kitchen. It was peaceful there and I felt whole that fall, resting my mind after Evergreen. I was mentally and emotionally preparing for a more rigorous and focused graduate program.

I was excited, yet feared I would not be good enough. I had to take a risk or my life and Nate's would never improve. All I wanted was for Nate to have a better life than my own.

In February, a few months before Nate's fifth birthday, I decided to visit an old boyfriend, Steve, who was living on San Juan Island. I packed Nate up and we drove north to Anacortes. The ferry parking lot was so much bigger than I was used to and the ticket cost way more than I expected. We drove down lane four in my Toyota wagon and waited for over an hour. We finally drove on the boat for the longest ferry ride ever. The boat stopped at Lopez, Shaw, Orcas, and finally San Juan. It took almost two and half hours.

I had heard about the islands from my dad when he was working for the energy assistance program there. He told stories about the hot tubs at the Elite hotel, listening to Country Joe once at Herb's Tavern, and the alder smoke smell of the cabin dwellers on Lopez.

When I was younger I had thought that Whidbey was the San Juans. I was surprised by their stunning beauty and the unusual topography and vegetation. The terrain reminded me of California with oak groves and dry grassy hills. I was enamored by the rocky shores and the high cliffs lined with tall fir trees and the rusty red bark peeling from the Madrona trees as they hung over the black rocky cliffs and the deep green sea.

Steve lived on Garrison Bay in a little one-room cabin off of Yacht Haven with only a hand pump for water and an outhouse. It was charming. We could see and smell the bay and there was a little stream-like inlet flowing deep into the woods by his cabin. There were five rentals on the property and I made friends right away with the other young hippie moms.

Nate and I took our showers at the health club that weekend and ate at Downriggers. I was captivated by this little place. It reminded me so much of Langley before the tourists came. It was funky, unpolished, and people still hung out in the mornings drinking coffee, eating steamed eggs and beer bread toast, reading the *Journal* and talking for hours at Front Street Cafe.

I had a strong feeling that I might be able to raise Nate in this little town. I could be a therapist here.

My life would be an open book.

I would have to walk my talk. It would be challenging. It would give me the parameters I needed and boundaries I had never had. It felt manageable for me as a young single mom. It felt safe.

The day before kindergarten started Nate and I moved in with Steve. Those first few months in the small cabin were hell. I moved Nate from everything and everyone he loved. I failed to understand what that would mean. Nate was angry and hurt. We didn't connect with his teacher and the relationship with Steve, once again, was not working out.

To make matters worse I found myself pregnant by the end of October. I was tormented by what to do. I wasn't willing to be a parent alone again. Steve was not ready to be a dad and our relationship was not strong enough to include a baby.

In order to save myself and to assure Nate had what he needed, I decided to have an abortion. It was awful. I was heartbroken because I loved being a mom. I loved babies. I loved being pregnant. But deep in my soul I knew it wasn't right to have another baby. It wasn't fair to anyone. I wouldn't be able to do it well. I could barely manage one child, let alone two.

I prayed for peace around my decision. I prayed for the spirit of that little baby to come back another time. It was not what I wanted. The pain of it was almost unbearable, but I did it anyway. Steve and I took the red-eye, and drove the two hours to a clinic in Seattle. All I saw as we drove down I-5 was road-kill. On the sides of the road there were dead raccoons, cats, deer, a dog, and an opossum.

The Protesters were outside with their signs and chants. The receptionist was covered in tattoos. The small, sterile room was cold and too quiet. My legs rested reluctantly in the metal stirrups. I carefully compartmentalized. I detached as they vacuumed the fetus from my womb.

I wanted to throw up.
I breathed.
I cried.
I breathed.

He drove to the ferry.
I slept.

By January I was pregnant again.

I hated myself.
I hated Steve.
I drove to the clinic, again, alone.

He cheated on me.
We broke up.
He left.

I moved into a bigger cabin, but with a longer path. I hauled my water in five gallon jugs, one in each hand, from my car down the trail to the cabin. We took short quarter-showers at the port and did laundry at Roche Harbor.

I drove to Seattle for school on Fridays. Asleep in my

arms, I delivered Nate to my neighbors, Rich, Linda and their daughter Megan's house, at five-thirty on Friday mornings. I drove to the ferry and then Seattle. I came back on the late boat, and at eleven at night I scooped Nate up off Linda's or my friend Liza's couch and brought him home to our little cabin.

I waitressed at the Bistro and cleaned houses to make ends meet. I volunteered at North Island's Mental Health. I was filing at first and I soon became an intern. It was there I learned how to be a therapist. The experienced therapists at the agency were welcoming and kind, and taught me what they knew. The director took me under his wing and guided me towards a psychodynamic training program at the University of Washington, which became the foundation of my psychotherapy work.

Within that program I learned how to analyze the therapeutic relationship. I learned how to use the relationship to help people heal their past relationships and grow in the present. I learned to listen for and give weight to the meaning of all that my clients brought me. I developed the ability to understand the patterns in people's stories and to find the unconscious thread that ran through their lives. I became skillful at interpretation and more aware of what actually helped on a deep, internal level, not simply on the surface. I practiced staying in the deepest ways I knew possible. I practiced and practiced.

EIGHT
Spring 2002

Nate has been at Anasazi for eight weeks. He writes and tells me about his life in the desert. He eats oatmeal that he cooks over a small fire for breakfast and rice for dinner, dried fruit and nuts for snacks. He drinks water from a canteen. He hikes during the day and sleeps outside at night. He learns how to survive with very little.

He trains himself not to need or want anything, and maybe not to care. Progress with his young female therapist is slow, if nonexistent. His letters home are dry, unemotional, short, and feel contrived. I hear what I perceive as the hate he has for me in every word of every letter.

I convince myself I am saving his life from meth and coke. But he feels abandoned, betrayed, and controlled. My decisions are careful and thoughtful.

I read A *Million Little Pieces*, by James Frey before I know anything about the questioned validity of the book, and it's all too familiar and oddly comforting. Reading this book is the only time I feel like someone might understand what I am going through. It is also helping me understand "Nate the addict."

A friend of mine who is a therapist and mother of a recovered heroin addict assures me that Nate's struggle with addiction is more painful for him than me, although it never feels that way. Her words help me have compassion.

I need compassion.

I breathe.

Nate stays an extra two weeks because, according to his counselor, he is not taking responsibility for his behavior. He is resistant and unwilling to admit he needs to quit using. He agrees to give up white substances, which means meth and cocaine.

I feel hopeful, like when you cross your fingers even though you know it won't make a difference, but I know in my heart he is still angry and in pain. I want to rebuild our relationship. I pray Nate knows how much I love him. I am grateful that Anasazi is, at least, keeping him alive.

I am unwilling to leave Vida in Friday Harbor, so my mom joins us to watch her. We fly down to Arizona to pickup Nate. My mom will stay with Vida at the hotel for one night while Larry and I join Nate in the desert. It is the first time I have left Vida overnight and it has been one year to the day since I picked her up that Saturday morning in Guatemala. I know today I have to put Nate first; it's not easy for me. I have made a small, laminated photo book for Vida about her one night with Grammy. I know she will be happy and okay, but it is still hard for me.

For one night in the desert Nate will share his outdoor life with us. He has been here two months. I can hardly digest the reality of that. It must have been hard for him to be hiking all day with very few amenities, while being pushed to his limits physically and emotionally.

We drive out to the beginning of a desert trail with an Anasazi staff person. The staff are young. We are with other middle-aged parents in the van. I am, predictably, the youngest. We are all nervous. We say very little to each other. We are ashamed. None of us know how our children will greet us. I pretend I am relaxed. We arrive at the trail head. We are led to Nate's campsite. There are cactus and sage everywhere. The earth beneath our feet is a reddish brown.

I see him. My heart beats faster and my breathing quickens. I take a deep breath.

He is thinner, tanner, and stronger. His eyes are bluer than ever. I haven't seen his eyes this clear in over a year. He wears a black t-shirt with the sleeves cut off. He has on his silver hoop earrings. He wears a Tibetan Buddhist mala around his neck. It is made from the bodhi seeds. My mom, a practicing Tibetan Buddhist, gave it to me a few years ago when she took me to a retreat at Spirit Rock. Nate took a liking to it. I was happy he wanted it.

His hair is grown out a bit from the time he shaved it and it's a little more brown than blond. His skin is as clear and brown. No more grey skin or open sores from the meth. His cheeks are a healthy pink on top of the golden brown from eight weeks outside. I see the light film of freckles across his nose and under his eyes that he has had since the summer he turned two. He has grown a thin blondish-red beard and mustache. His muscles are defined. He is muscular, handsome, and confident. The sunlight through the desert shrubbery illuminates his glow.

We hug.

It is a cold hug.

He is not ready.

I can't help the tears streaming down my face. It is hard for both of us. Everything is not better.

Nate is guarded. I struggle to keep my heart open, but inside it's breaking because the distance between us is unbearable. Despite the barriers between us, I can at least see that my Nate is here.

He is present.

He is in his body.

He is gentler than when I left him.

He is healthier.

I breathe.

I am quiet, taking him in. What is he thinking? Feeling? I have no idea what to say or do. I try and follow his lead, to listen and to pay attention to him. He is quiet. Cautious.

Larry talks. He asks questions about the terrain, the food, the equipment, etc. Nate answers. He's not going to tell me how he feels or what he is thinking. I don't really blame him.

Maybe he doesn't even know. I hope that will come later. At least for now, we are here in the desert together and he is not on meth.

He is alive.

I breathe, again.

He cooks for us over a small open campfire that he starts with flint and shavings of dry kindling. He shows us the sticks he has whittled to use as spoons for stirring and eating. We eat from the enamel cups we have been instructed to bring. He allows me to take his photo and is especially proud of his flat stomach and tanned body. He tells us how he once tried to leave and hiked to the highway to get a steak from a diner. He wanted to run away.

He almost did.

But he didn't.

Here he is.

He tells us about his solo time and how he didn't learn that much. He explains that living without the comforts of home, screens, friends, etc. didn't really bother him. He tells me that he learned that none of those things really matter and that he doesn't need them to be happy.

We eat rice for dinner, boiled over the campfire, and sleep in our sleeping bags in the shelter he has made for us. We listen to the same night sounds he has listened to for eight weeks. We look up at the same stars. We wake up in the morning and he makes us oatmeal, again, over the fire. We eat with our carved sticks from our gray enamel cups.

After breakfast we hike out and meet the Anasazi van. After photos with the other families we head back to the Anasazi office and Nate is officially discharged. He wears a red bandana tied around his head.

In his exit summary with his therapist, Nate will not agree to quit drinking and drugging. He says again he will quit the white stuff, coke and meth, but not alcohol or pot. He is being honest. I am afraid that our journey through hell is not even close to being over.

I feel sick.

I feel scared.

I hold my breath.

At the hotel, my brother Oliver joins us. I begged him to come. I am putting a lot of pressure on him to show up for Nate, physically and emotionally. We have been having long, heated discussions about his relationship with Nate and my fear that all the men in Nate's life are not invested enough. My brother tries to be patient with me. He has difficulty understanding what I am going through as a mom. He doesn't have children yet. He is unfamiliar with Nate's rebelliousness and addiction issues.

Oliver is not like this.

My Dad didn't even consider coming to Arizona. He blames me most of the time for Nate's problems. He tells me the things he doesn't like about Larry and questions our marriage. He doubts my parenting style. He thinks I am too lenient. He thinks, as always, I should be different than I am. It doesn't seem to matter what I do; it is never good enough and he never approves. I feel judged by everyone in my family. They judge my parenting, my decision making, and my marriage. I judge and blame myself, too. I either shut down in silence or scream until I am in tears trying to communicate with my family. I want them to understand and to help. I feel like I am being nailed to a cross in every conversation.

I am exhausted.

I know we are all scared and just want someone to blame. We are looking for a reason and a way to fix Nate's addiction. No one is actually holding Nate accountable for his choices or his behavior.

I want Nate's dad to show up. I call him crying, yelling, blaming, confronting him about his own addictions, about his son's need of him, but to no avail. He either hangs up on me or is conveniently unavailable the next time I call.

I am furious. He has let Nate down a million times. My heart aches thinking about all the times he said he would pick

Nate up or come to one of Nate's football or baseball games. We would watch and wait for him. Nate would look over at the clock or from the field to the sideline, his eyes saying "Where's my dad?" Every minute of that was brutal for me and even more brutal for Nate.

I explain addiction to Nate when he is seven and his dad has failed to show up, again. He calls with some excuse about missing the ferry, sleeping in at some woman's house in Tacoma. I always know this means he is hungover from drinking or has been up all night using cocaine. I explain to Nate his dad struggles with addiction, that I think he's an alcoholic, and that none of his dad's behaviors are Nate's fault.

Over the years, I send Glen pamphlets from AA about addiction to his post office box in Dutch Harbor. I ask him to send Nate a letter explaining his addiction and telling Nate it is not Nate's fault. To his credit, he does. Perhaps that helps a little, but still Nate waits for his dad to show up, all the time, everywhere. Addiction is confusing.

Nate watches Larry show up for his older kids and now for Vida. He watches my dad show up for Oliver and his stepson Jonah. My dad showed up when Nate was little, but it's harder for him now that Nate is older. As inadequate as I am, at least I show up.

We stay together that night in the hotel in Arizona, wondering if anything will be better and feeling all our relationships are a little broken. I feel like the only one who sees this as a family problem. Everyone else sees it as Nate's problem, or my problem. I imagine Nate feels he is on his own.

I feel I am on my own, too.

Once we are home, Nate returns to Friday Harbor High School and tries out for the baseball team. We have some semblance of normalcy. We celebrate his seventeenth birthday six weeks after returning from Anasazi. He feels far away. He is detached.

He doesn't really look me in the eye. He avoids conversation with me. It's as if he is a robot going through the motions. But there is no real emotion. When others laugh, he laughs. When he is asked questions, he answers with the bare minimum. I no longer know him and that is the way he wants it.

Our relationship is awkward. I don't know how to relate to him. The way before drugs, before Vida, before he started hating me, is no longer an option. I am edgy. I am hypervigilant. I am unsure.

He is sober.

I hold my breath.

NINE

August 1967

My parents were married just eight months before I was born. It was December 28, 1966. My mom, Mully, was six weeks pregnant with me. They had been having an on-and-off-again relationship. When they married it was under a certain amount of duress, but it was the expectation of the time, and of their parents. Mully was twenty-one and Skip had just turned twenty-two.

She wore a short, white lace, A-line dress with a high collar. My mom has always loved the high collar, the turtle neck, and the mandarin collar. She wore the daisy chain she made in her mousey brown hair. It was curled under in somewhat of a bob and she had a long side-part bang sweeping her forehead. She looked darling, as my Auntie Barb would say.

My dad wore a black suit, maroon tie, and white button-up shirt. He still had hair, although the Demuth receding hairline was already prominent. His hair was dark, almost black, and cut relatively short.

It was a small and quaint ceremony. Fourteen people in all. A Unitarian minister married them in a very small, plain meeting room with a few flowers on the table. The minister read the Kahlil Gibran poem on marriage.

Within a few months, my mom dyed her wedding dress a golden orange, and they sold all their wedding presents, including a box of genuine silverware for $200 to someone in San Francisco, who'd answered their ad in the newspaper. My Grandma Natalie and Auntie Barb were horrified, since it had been their gift.

My parents no longer valued material things. They had no interest in conforming to the bourgeoisie. They used the money from selling their wedding presents and they traded in their VW Beetles for a navy blue 1967 Volkswagen bus with a sliding side door and white trim.

That hot, dry summer in Davis, California, my parents lived in a little cottage tucked away in a back alley off D Street. The rent was seventy-eight dollars a month. The previous renter was an artist who became a Buddhist monk. His name was Dan Welsh. Dan had painted murals on the walls. The bedroom was painted with white clouds in the style of Magritte, and a six-foot silver lightning bolt was hanging on the living room wall. The bathroom was painted silver as well.

My mom loved that little cottage and fixed it up sweetly with garage-sale furniture, rugs, dishes, and knickknacks as she prepared to welcome me into the world. She found my white wicker bassinet at a garage sale and wove white tulle and satin ribbons through it. She added beads, bells, and feathers throughout.

Most days she walked in the scorching Davis heat down the street a few blocks to a friend's apartment building that had a pool. My mom loved swimming. She wore her navy blue maternity swimsuit covered in little white daisies with yellow centers. Her hair was wound up off her shoulders in a clip. She wore navy blue saltwater sandals on her bare feet. Swimming was a relief from the heat and the weight of her third-trimester belly. My mom had not gained much weight, so she was mostly belly.

It was 1967, the Summer of Love. My dad had just completed his bachelor of arts at UC Davis and my mom had dropped a class, so she was just a few credits shy from receiving her degree in early childhood development. Just over an hour south, one-hundred-thousand long-haired hippies had converged in the Haight-Ashbury neighborhood of San Francisco. The city had become a melting pot of politics, music, drugs, creativity, and a total lack of sexual and social inhibition. The civil rights movement was afoot, the Vietnam War protests were growing and on the horizon was the birth of the women's movement.*

Skip and Mully were anti-establishment; they were against the bourgeoisie, the rich, the white male politicians, and anything or anyone status quo. They were radical political hippies and they wanted to make a difference. They wanted to change the world.

My dad was given a fellowship to the University of Washington's doctorate program in political science. He hoped to one day be a professor and affect change in the minds of young people. We were off to Seattle in the navy blue VW bus.

I was three weeks old.

During those sixteen months in Seattle, my mom and I were inseparable. She dressed me in the sweetest of hand-embroidered and floral-print dresses, as well as her signature overalls, which she adorned with patches and detailed embroidery, light blue with little white daisies, red corduroy, and engineer striped Oshkosh. On my chubby wrist I wore ten colorful teeny enamel bracelets that Patty, my mom's best friend since kindergarden, had brought back from India.

My mom wore her hair in pig tails and braids. Her warm smile went well with her collection of handmade smock tops, long jean shorts, worn-out embroidered overalls, hippie dresses, and bare feet.

She was a proud mom. She and my dad carted me to Student's for a Democratic Society (SDS) meetings on campus and anti-war protests in downtown Seattle. I was the rare baby at these political meetings and peace marches full of college students.

My mom knit teeny baby parkas and made beaded jewelry. She laid them out on my baby blankets and sold them on the sidewalk in the "U-District." She was always thinking, challenging and being political in her own right. She valued being my mother and she raised me to be an empowered girl. She wanted me to have equal rights to men and boys.

My mom bought my baby buggy at the thrift store for a

dollar. Sometimes at the grocery store she would tuck a little block of swiss cheese under my blankets and leave without paying. Other times when she went to the drug store to pick up photos for my dad, she would slip the envelope under my blanket and leave without paying. My dad documented our lives with his camera. The black-and-whites he printed himself and the color ones he took to the drug store.

They were living on two hundred dollars a month. They moved into a bigger house on Roosevelt and their rent increased. Sometimes the GIs from McChord Air Force Base in Tacoma came down and stayed at our house for the weekend. They talked about the government and the war in Vietnam, and my parents provided a place for the GI's to sleep and take a break from the oppressive rigors of the military.

My mom ventured out with me from the U-District to Pike Place Market where she discovered artists in the basement. We hung out there many days and she sold her hand-knit baby parkas and jewelry with the other hippies and artists. On sunnier days we rode the bus to Greenlake, swam, and walked around the lake.

One weekend my parents took a day trip to explore the greater Seattle area. They drove north up I-5 to Mount Vernon and made their way through the Skagit Valley and La Conner. My mom stopped and bought some local honey on Best Road. Driving back to Seattle they took the scenic route over Deception Pass Bridge and down Whidbey Island. They passed the entrance to the Oak Harbor Naval Base with its fighter plane on display and where the sign to the entrance read: Pardon Our Noise. It's the Sound of Freedom.

My mom loved the tall fir trees and arching alders that lined the roads of Whidbey. We rode the Rhododendron ferry, which I later came to call "the hot chocolate ferry" because it had a galley. My mom wrapped me in the yellow blanket she had knit, held me out on the deck of the ferry, and showed me the Puget Sound, the seagulls, and the little islands. The ride was twenty-five minutes from Clinton to Mukilteo.

When I was about five months old, my mom and dad, and I went to Eagles Hall, a well-known place for hearing rock and roll music in Seattle. The Grateful Dead were playing. My mom went into the kitchen on the break and Jerry Garcia was in there getting a glass of water.

I was in her arms. She was concerned about the volume of the music on my ears.

She asked Jerry if he thought the music was going to hurt my ears. He said "Oh no, my daughter, Sunshine, comes to all of our rehearsals, she listens to all our music and her hearing is fine." My mom was comforted by his response.

She thanked him, fed me, rocked me back to sleep and stayed for the second set.

Another day my mom picked up Malvina Reynolds in the VW bus at Sea-Tac Airport, and transported her to her concert venue. Leslie, my mom's closest friend in Seattle, went along for the ride. They were becoming close and spent many days together in the city.

Malvina was a folksinger whose songs my mom often sang to me. "Little Boxes" was her favorite, and mine.

Country Joe came to Seattle for a peace march. My parents and I went to the march downtown. Country Joe and the Fish were playing on the back of a flatbed truck and helped lead the march. My mom was involved in the Women's Strike for Peace, which helped organize the march. Country Joe and the Fish were well known already for the Fish Cheer.

"Give me an F! Give me a U! Give me a C! Give me a K!"

"What's that spell? What's that spell?"

It's the introduction to his famous song "Fixin' to Die Rag" about the American soldiers fighting in the Vietnam War. Joe himself had already been in the service and wore his army-issued jacket. My mom made a connection with Joe's music.

During the years in Seattle my parents met Robby Stern. He was in law school at UW when they met. He was outspoken and driven by his experience being raised Jewish in the black south. He and my parents, along with Leslie, were political friends and cohorts. Robby was the leader of SDS on the UW campus.

My dad finished his master's degree in December 1968. We drove the VW bus to Wenatchee, where my Dad had accepted a job teaching political science at Wenatchee Valley Community College.

Wenatchee was a conservative little town, full of apple orchards and mostly rednecks. It was still insulated from the radical political ideas of the young hippies protesting in the big cities around much of the country.

My parents began having late-night meetings at our little white house. The few black students and interested white students hung out with my parents as they discussed Vietnam, civil rights, and the right-wing establishment.

They'd pass a joint around and talk about their ideas. My mom always skipped the pot. She went with the contact high, that was enough for her. I woke up late in the night and came out of my room to listen and soak up the attention of the young passionate students in my living room.

The students and my dad organized a sit-in protesting the presence of ROTC on campus. My dad showed films about the Black Panthers as well as providing other empowering educational materials.

They then refused to leave the administrative offices on the college campus. My mom didn't attend the sit-in, but she and I did bring fried chicken to the students, handed it to them through the window, and said hello. Later my mom and I made a chocolate cake and delivered it through the window, too. The Wenatchee police came as well, but not for the cake.

Two of the students were men my parents had become good friends with. Quincy and Mack had spent a lot of time with us. They were tall black men who came to Wenatchee to play basketball for the community college. This small, mostly white conservative town did not embrace these black men, but my parents did. The administration could not be swayed. The *Wenatchee World* covered the story. My dad was asked to leave the college and agreed to offer him a good recommendation, if he left peacefully.

It was May, the quarter hadn't quite ended, but my parents held a garage sale on the front lawn. They sold my bouncy horse and almost everything else we owned. We were all packed up, Quincy, Mack, and a local boy named Stu included. We were headed in the VW bus down the familiar freeway south to Berkeley.

I was not even two.

* Facts quoted from Wikipedia, 2016

TEN

Summer 2002

By the time high school prom passes in May, Nate is back to using regularly. I don't think it's meth, maybe just alcohol and pot.

I try not to think about it.

I clench my teeth.

I try to give him boundaries and choices. I set up work for him, but he doesn't really want to work. He reluctantly helps our friend Malcom with a construction project at his house. Everything about being his mom is hard. It is painful and just plain scary. I am ineffective and uptight. He is noncompliant and detached.

I talk to Don.

I talk to Jan.

I talk to June.

I talk with an old family friend from Whidbey. She is a psychiatric nurse and her son was in a head on collision while playing chicken on an old side road. The kids were under the influence. He is now dead. He was only eighteen. It happened two weeks after his high school graduation. His mom has one piece of encouragement for me: as long as Nate is alive there is hope. I hang on to her words. I repeat her words more times than I ever thought imaginable.

As long as he is alive, there is hope.

As long as he is alive, there is hope.

As long as he is alive, there is hope.

I focus on Vida. I hang out with her reading dozens of books, cooking, singing, and taking long walks down Lampard Road. I look forward to my mom's group. Sometimes we meet at our house or at another mom's house. When it's sunny we meet at Eagle Cove.

Eagle Cove has been my favorite place ever since an old boyfriend first brought me here with his kids in 1991. Nate was seven. It's magical. The trail down to the beach is overgrown with alders, nettles, Queen Anne's Lace, and horsetails. There is a small creek to the left as you walk down, which keeps the trail lush and green. Walking down the hill and emerging from the trail, you can see the beach as it takes you out past the rocks on a minus tide. It's breathtaking every time.

My heart always stops at the beauty of this protected and quiet cove that only the locals visit. It got its name, of course, from the bald eagles that fly above, and if you are lucky on some days, the orca whales swim by and breech. On a clear day the jagged Olympic Mountains are visible with little white caps left from the winter's snow. The water is shallow forever, so children can play safely, running and jumping over the small waves on the soft sand, which is rare for our island beaches. They splash each other, pushing driftwood into the water to make boats and rafts.

Eagle Cove is sacred.

Today is one of many lazy days at Eagle Cove. I am only working two days a week, so most days Vida and I can arrive early with our blanket and snacks. The tide is usually way out and we are typically alone the first hour. Around eleven the other mothers and babies arrive.

The babies run naked in the tidepools and waves. They climb the rocks, look for crabs, and find prickly sea anemones. We talk about all the joys, trials, and tribulations of raising children. They know some of my struggles with Nate. They see my pain and grief. I can't hide it, though I am still quite private and don't share too much. They are all first-time moms and have little in the way of guidance to offer, but they listen. I am grateful that they are always kind.

The teenagers and twenty-somethings typically show up around two o'clock with music, beer, cigarettes, skimboards, and bocce ball. Sometimes Nate's friends are among them. I am flooded with grief. Vida and I head up the path for home then. She is ready for a nap.

I'm tired, too.

I do my best to protect the sacredness of life for Vida while Nate spirals out of control, again. School is out and he moves to his dad's on Whidbey. Two weeks later, he is home after a physical confrontation with his dad. He is using, of course. He won't follow his dad's rules either and he and his dad have very little patience for each other.

When he comes home I try to act normal, to have expectations, but also to give him freedom; it is all ineffective. One night in August, the night before he is supposed to get his tonsils out, I get a call at four in the morning. He has crashed my car on Beaverton Valley Road. He is okay; my car is not. I postpone the surgery.

He starts his senior year at Friday Harbor High School. But he drops out of Friday Harbor High School. He can't follow the rules. I help him move to Mount Vernon, where he attends Running Start at Skagit Valley College. He doesn't attend class and wants to move to Lopez Island and live with a friend. Lopez is just a ferry ride away and I am not in favor. But he does what he wants and I no longer have any control. He enrolls at Lopez High School.

It's only been six months since he returned from the desert. My head is spinning. Every move I am packing, driving, and paying. I am run down, afraid, and losing hope. He is using. I don't know what he's using. But I know this is all using behavior.

How much should I give him?

How much should I care about him or what he does?

Is it worth it?

He doesn't seem to care at all.

But I know this can't be true.

While Nate is moving to Lopez, Vida is turning two. We are building a new house. We have sold the yurts to a couple on Orcas. When we move into our new house, a sweet family from Orcas deconstructs the huge deck and the four yurts that have been our home for eleven years.

We have bought a three-bedroom modular home, which we are moving onto a different building site on our five acres. I'm excited about living in a real house. A house that looks clean when you clean it. A house that holds in the heat, instead of letting it out through the thin canvas and lattice walls. I have been dreaming of this day since Nate was a baby. My own real and new house with wood floors, sheetrock walls, big windows facing the sun, two bathrooms, a large kitchen, and a sprawling deck.

No more rustic cabins or yurts.

No more funkiness.

It's a house I can be in for the rest of my life. It's a house my children and grandchildren will be able to come back to and visit for years to come.

I am consumed with the details of the house while planning Vida's second birthday and trying to keep track of Nate. I call him and leave messages at the places he is staying, but he doesn't call me back. When I do see him, it's usually because he needs something, and he feels detached from me, more distant than ever before. It's like there is an invisible barrier between us that I cannot penetrate.

I am slowly giving up on trying to influence him, or parent him. I do my best to stay in some kind of relationship with him. I hope he will eventually choose health and the love of his family over drugs.

I call him once a week on Lopez. I ask him not to live on Lopez, but he refuses to come home. I call the mother of the teenage boy he is living with and ask her to send him home. I tell her he does not have my permission to live with her. I tell her I will not give him or her any money to live there. I call the school counselor and tell her my concerns. Nothing I do changes the reality that he is living on Lopez. Nothing changes the reality that he is living without me.

I feel sick.

I breathe.

I include him in the process of designing the new house. I want him to help paint his room. I want him to live in the new house with us. He is angry and resentful. He barely participates.

"Now you get a new house?" he says.

"Now that I am almost an adult?"

"Vida gets to have a house?"

"A real house."

"I had to live in the yurts?"

I understand.

I know this feeling.

"I'm sorry," I tell him, but it's not enough.

I can't fix it.

I cry.

I have let him down, again.

How could I have been so stupid?

How could I have not known?

I invite him and his new girlfriend to Vida's birthday. She lives on Lopez, too. Her mother is a nurse. I'm horrified that my drug-addicted, seventeen-year-old son is dating her fourteen-year-old daughter. I call her mom to let her know I am aware and I do not approve of the situation. I explain to her it's out of my control. I tell her I'm sorry. She is kind, but not happy.

All of Vida's two-year-old friends come to her party. We pile into two cars and drive to the horse ranch on San Juan Valley Road and take very slow, epic, circular pony rides. Vida is the happiest. She loves horses.

Back at the house we have a piñata, my dad's secret-recipe chocolate mayonnaise cake and vanilla ice cream. Nate helps Vida with the piñata. He is in good spirits and it seems he is not using. I'm happy to see him. I like his girlfriend. Maybe he will be okay.

I hope.

I breathe.

By November, Nate is playing on the basketball team for Lopez. It is a small team and with his height and athleticism, he is a helpful addition. Vida and I take the ferry to Lopez to see as many games as we can. I change my work appointments so that I can make it to his games. I know some of the kids and parents on Lopez from working here ten years ago.

I remember one little girl in particular. We took long walks instead of staying in the office. One spring, we walked and picked the tiny pink buds off the Nootka rose bushes on the side of the road. Gathering as many as we could in a little basket, we carried them back to the office and strung them with a needle, through the little green hip, on a thread. There were at least one hundred on each rosary, and we wore them around our necks. That sweet little girl had taught me how to make a beautiful, fragrant rosary from the wild Nootka rose and still each spring I think of her as I walk Lampard Road picking those tiny pink buds. I carefully string them and place the fragrant buds around my neck and remember her.

Now I am worried about Nate developing friendships, having sex, or doing drugs with former female clients, maybe even that little girl who is only a few years younger than he is. What must the school counselor think of me as a mom? As a therapist? And what must the other parents think of me now that my son is living on Lopez, without a parent or guardian?

I know on some level Nate is on Lopez because he is trying to protect me from his dangerous choices. He even tells me this once. He knows if he did this in Friday Harbor, it would be even more painful to me.

Vida and I visit the home where Nate is living. The driveway is messy and the property looks run down. There are pieces of farm equipment lying around. I walk into the laundry room entry and there are empty cardboard boxes piled on the washing machine. There are dirty clothes, baskets, and more boxes piled all over the filthy floor.

I hate it.

I go further into the room that Nate is sharing with his friend. It's a basement room with windows. There are liquor bottles all along the windowsills, more than I can count. There are clothes strewn all around the room on the floor and every surface. There is garbage mixed in with the clothes and liquor bottles. It smells dirty, sweaty, and like cigarettes and rotting food.

I am enraged.

I am disgusted.

I feel sick.

Again.

I tell him that I don't want him living like this. He tells me the mom is nice, and that it's not as bad as it looks. I shake my head and we head to the village for dinner. I don't get into it. Later I hear a rumor that the mom is addicted to painkillers.

My Lopez visits are like this throughout basketball season. It rains, a lot. We meet another family with a little girl; Grace is Vida's age and is also adopted. Grace's mom is a Christian. She is kind. I try to relax. I try not to feel so bad.

Nate looks good. He seems sober and is making good grades. I give him five to ten dollars each time I see him. It's an offering of some support, but not enough to enable unhealthy choices.

I ask him to come home, but still he refuses

ELEVEN

Everyday

I can feel the blame on me like a wool blanket, too heavy, weighing me down, suffocating me. I blame myself for being a teenage mother. I blame myself for having a son with a man whose drug and alcohol use was already a problem for me and I assumed even then would be a problem for a long time. I blame myself for every problem and every struggle Nate has had.

I try to teach him to take responsibility. I make him write long apology letters for vandalizing a porta-potty at the baseball field with some friends when he is twelve years old. I insist he does his homework. I limit TV time. I enforce regular bedtimes. I provide healthy food. I keep the house clean. I wash, dry, and fold all the laundry every week. I take care of everything I know how to take care of. No matter what I do, I never feel like I am quite a good-enough mother.

I have to stop. I forgive myself a little bit every day. I say to myself, *you did the best you could with what you had.* I remember what I have done that was good enough.

Even though I didn't plan to get pregnant, I chose to take care of my baby. My face is wet with tears and my heart aches knowing how much I wanted to protect him, love him, never drop him, and never leave him. I am flooded by memories every day. His first baby blanket, which I sewed for him was white flannel with little red, blue, and green cars scattered on it and navy blue satin trim, which I had no idea how to sew on, but I did anyway. It was always a bit crooked.

Instead of thinking about the nights I was tired and stressed and let him cry in his crib, I think about the many more nights that I scooped him up and rocked him and walked him until he fell asleep.

I think about the songs I sang to him every night from the first day he was born until he was at least ten years old; "Twinkle, Twinkle Little Star," "Favorite Things," and "Circle Game." I sang each and every word.

I remember the good and healthy choices Nate has made over the years. I remember all the baseball, football, and soccer games he played from the time he was six years old. I remember his love of math and his sense of humor. I love thinking about the times it was just him and me driving, joking, and talking. All the time we've had in this life, just him and me.

I can't help but laugh when I think of the time June and I took him and his friend Adrian camping with us at the Gorge for Lilith Fair. They were fourteen. It was one-hundred degrees and they were surrounded by thousands of sweaty, barely dressed women, half of whom were lesbians.

I am comforted when I think about the time for Mother's Day he framed a black-and-white photo of him and me, and over-layed the lyrics from "Momma's Song" by Tupac on the photo. I cried. I remember the three times he went to the ten-day Power of Hope camp in high school. Even when he had first begun using meth, even when he was angry, he went to Power of Hope.

Once at a Power of Hope songwriting camp, the year he had been living on Lopez, he wrote a hip-hop song for me. When he gave it to me he said, this is your gift for a while, Mom. I listen to it when I am missing him and losing hope.

For the ladies that make the babies.
We come from them.
Then we run from them.

Got a name from a woman.
Got a game from a woman.
We love them, we love them.

We raise them, then they raise us.
No matter what our actions come back to us.
It's a battle, we need a damn reason.
No need to play a role, you need to love the women.
Love your children, no more slugs and dealin.'

Smile for me,
Because I used to smile for you.
Give me everything,
Because I love you.

Momma this is for you,
You the light of my life.
When the Earth grows cold,
You make the fire bright.

I've done wrong things,
Once, twice or more.
But I am apologizing to you,
No more war.

Single mom going to school, just seventeen.
Can't even imagine struggles in my wildest dreams.
Can you even compare what you overcome,
You, on your own, raisin' a son.

My mom made do
when she made ends meet.
Kept food keep on grindin'
Between my teeth.

So sad, no, I'm happy,
I don't cry, I weep,
Make my heart thump,
Make the hits beat.
Enjoy, they so low, they drop so far.

They warm like the sun,
I am so glad I'm your son.
In the days I was sick you always made me better.
The cloudiest days, ma, you changed the weather.

And together we will be, until death do us part,
Momma you are my soul, locked up in my heart.
So maybe one day I could pray that you smile,
Love what I done, your first born child.

That's how I remember. Like a river, flowing one after another into the next. Every time a memory comes to me I forgive myself a little bit. Each time, I hand Nate's life back to him; I have done all I can do, except let go.

Really let go.

I am not very good at letting go, so maybe no one can tell that I am trying. I promise, I am. Teeny tiny bits at a time, immeasurable really, but it will add up. Because if I can save myself from this nasty stench of addiction, maybe Nate can save himself, too.

Or, maybe God can save him.

TWELVE

Winter 1970

After my dad lost his job in Wenatchee, we stayed with friends in the Bay Area. First we stayed with Bill Samsel in Berkeley, then Patty and Sandy in San Francisco. Patty had just given birth to Toby, her first baby, and a few years later would give birth to twins, a girl and a boy, named Tara and Kelsey.

Between couch surfing, my parents packed up the VW bus and we went camping in Yosemite. They made it back to Berkeley just in time for a huge protest march. The radicals were protesting the University of California at Berkeley because they had shut down People's Park a couple of weeks before. Everyone at the march was singing Beatles songs, Woody Guthrie's "This Land Is Your Land," and yelling anti-establishment chants. After what started as a peaceful march, it turned bloody and violent.

We still didn't have a house, so we stayed with my Auntie Barb in Oakland, on Trestle Glen. My dad flew to Chicago with Robby for a SDS meeting. The SDS was a group started by Tom Hayden in Michigan. The Weatherman Organization ended up growing out of a split from SDS. It was an intense gathering. The discussions were focused on the best way to make change in the US government. There was a lot of dissent. My dad returned politically energized.

We moved in with some friends my parents met through the want ads. Our new house was just blocks away from the Peoples Park Annex. The annex was a small piece of land in the city that the people started using when UC Berkeley shut down Peoples Park. My mom and Jerry, one of our roommates, built a little play house at the park. They used a little red flyer wagon to haul the building materials. All the hippie kids at the park helped, ran around naked in the sun, and played in the dirt.

Living with Jerry, Beth, and their daughter Rachel didn't last long. In October my parents heard about the Working Class Organizing Collective, a group that used concepts developed by Karl Marx to drive their activism. They organized the working class by going into the workplace and becoming one with the workers, while educating them about the need for change in the government. My parents and I and eleven other couples in their early to mid-twenties moved to San Leandro. They worked in the factories and educated the workers and young people.

My dad worked at the Kellogg's factory with another activist named Bob. He was on the line that put the raisins in Kellogg's Raisin Bran. My mom audited a class at the junior college. Robby and Leslie, from Seattle, were part of the collective and lived in a house with us in San Leandro. They were all attending meetings and talking to high school students, college students, and other young people about the atrocities of the Vietnam War, capitalism, and the general corruption in the US government.

Everything was anti-establishment.

Robby worked in a factory, too. Leslie and my mom spent a lot of time together handing out flyers, discussing ideas, and fighting for the movement. My mom made friends with the two other mothers in the collective, Linda and René.

Linda had two children, a son little older than me and a daughter exactly my age, Kenny and Krissy. René had a baby boy named Huey, after Huey Newton, the cofounder, with Bobby Seale, of the Black Panther Party in 1966.

Everything was political.

Although my mom was fully immersed in the politics of the time and the Collective, her main focus was loving and caring for me. She drove me to a little preschool in Hayward in the VW bus and then she handed out flyers and engaged in her political work.

My parents attended meetings at Linda's house, which was bigger than ours and could accommodate all twenty-four members of the collective, as well as us four children. Linda kept a bag of chocolate chips and Cheerios with her at all times to feed to us, so we wouldn't interrupt the meetings. Mostly we played outside in the sandbox.

During the winter months recruiters came from the Weatherman Organization. They came from the East Coast to check out this young group of activists in San Leandro they had heard about. The recruiters were exploring their interest in joining their movement. They were expanding their collectives to the West Coast and looking for interested, like minded, committed young activists.

The Weathermen Organization believed in creating chaos inside the belly of the beast, the US government being the beast. The Weatherman Organization mission was to stop the Vietnam War, fight against imperialism, and change the fundamental way the United States functioned. In a nutshell, they wanted to end capitalism.

The Weathermen Organization was aggressive and insistent on their points of view. Both my parents were sympathetic to their analysis of the world and the US government. The Weatherman who were at the meeting, were well-known leaders of the movement. They were very smart and committed to direct action and confrontation. Rather than working quietly and respectfully to change people's minds, they wanted to infiltrate in an explosive way.

All around the Bay Area, young people were being attacked and shot by police. The sidewalks were lined with police in combat uniforms. They carried plastic shields, gas masks, billy sticks, and tear gas during the peace marches. It was happening all over the country. The political climate was volatile, to say the least. Emotions in the collective were running high. Regardless, my mom still took me to Mrs. Ting's little preschool up the hill in Hayward.

Everything was chaotic. Life and politics were moving

fast. Amidst the chaos my parents, Leslie and Robby, René and Joe decided to join the Weatherman. Children weren't allowed.

We were all going to be separated.

Bob and Barbara, a couple that had been living in San Leandro and working in the collective, had been setting up a house on Bocano Street in San Francisco. They were going to take care of baby Huey and me while our parents went underground to change the world.

In a matter of a day, my mom packed up as many of my things as she could. She dressed me in my Oshkosh overalls and my little red Keds, and prepared to leave me.

Bob and Barbara came in their Volvo to pick me up. My mom and dad told me they loved me and that they would come back to get me. It was February, and I had no idea when I would see my mom again.

Huey and I were left behind.

THIRTEEN

Spring 2003

Nate moves into a different house on Lopez.
He is working construction, some days.
He is secretive.
He is reserved.
He has money.
I assume he is selling pot and other drugs.

Matt, Larry's youngest son, visits Nate.
Nate has a gun.
He shows Matt the gun.

Matt comes to our house.
He tells us about the gun.

Before I know about the gun, I take his senior photos at Odlin Park. It's a beautiful campground and park. There is driftwood and a sandy beach. He looks good. Maybe it's not so bad on Lopez. Maybe he's not so bad with the drugs. This is just my denial, but I want it so bad to be true.

We go through the motions and act as if he is okay. He lets me take his senior photos. He doesn't smile much. He knows this is important to me, so he indulges me.

As I take his photos I see the tiny baby that I gave birth to eighteen years ago. The memories of our life together, especially the years before Larry, run through my mind like a movie. I can hear his laughs, see his tricks, see our hours of playing catch anywhere from the ferry line to the nearest baseball field, and, all the times I held his hand and rocked him in my arms. It takes all of me not to cry.

I drop him off at his new girlfriend's house and head back to the ferry landing. In my car, on the ferry, I can cry. I am grieving his childhood and all that has passed. The future does not seem as bright. I wonder what I have done wrong. I think about all the mistakes I have made over the years. I think again about the times I yelled, the times I didn't listen, the times I didn't understand.

I start making his graduation announcements. I print fifty small black-and-white photos of him squatting on the driftwood beach at Odlin Park, his shaved head, and big, strong shoulders pulling on his button-up shirt. His white undershirt is peeking out from beneath. He looks like a man. He looks sharp. He looks capable.

His grades have been pretty good at Lopez High School. He is still aloof, but I am patient. I think one day he will be himself with me again. And yet, even when things start to seem better, I can't help myself, I am still waiting for the other shoe to drop.

I hope it doesn't.

I wait.

It does.

Nate calls two weeks before graduation to tell me he won't be graduating. I have just addressed and stamped all the envelopes with announcements carefully placed inside. He has been caught plagiarizing his final senior English paper. He can't fix it before graduation and he is not permitted to walk with his class. He acts like he doesn't care.

"Fuck them," he says.

"I'll finish it later."

I am heartbroken.

I am speechless.

It's been over a year and a half of this addiction. I miss my son. I have been anticipating his graduation from high school for eighteen years; I had been hoping his experience could be different than mine, and, now it won't be happening. All of his friends and classmates from Friday Harbor will be graduating too. I will have to attend and I will have to watch the long-awaited slideshow that features each graduate from birth to graduation. Nate will be missing from that slideshow and the one at Lopez High School.

I cry.

I feel sick.

I feel ripped off.

I feel hopeless.

I lay down on the wood floor in my kitchen, curl up in a fetal position, and close my eyes.

One of my oldest friends from Evergreen is visiting me with her three-year-old daughter. They are up from Southeast Portland for the weekend when I find out about the gun. I am terrified. Michelle is terrified. It's like we've walked into the wrong theater. We went to see a feel-good movie about the magic of childhood and now we are watching Quentin Tarantino and someone is about to get shot in the head and thrown in the trunk.

I fear for Nate's life.

I fear for anyone's life who is in his proximity.

If he's drinking or doing drugs, who knows what could happen with a gun?

Who knows what he could do?

Who knows who could get killed?

I ask Larry to go to Lopez and get the gun from Nate. He takes the inter-island ferry to Lopez first thing the next morning. He comes back six hours later with the gun. Nate wouldn't just give it to him. Larry finally ended up buying the gun from Nate for $500. Larry wraps up the gun and hides it in a box on the highest shelf of the barn.

I am relieved.

I breathe, sort of.

Vida feels my stress. She bites my friend's daughter. I am

impatient. I am defensive. My friend is upset. My friend can't begin to imagine what I am going through. I am resentful that she is not more compassionate toward me. She protects her daughter and herself. I protect Vida. I try and protect Nate.

No one protects me.

I snap at my friend's daughter for not sitting at the table. I snap at her for getting sand on the blanket at Eagle Cove. I can't handle anything that is out of my control.

My friend and I have a fight. Harsh words are spoken. Tears are shed. Voices are raised. This has never happened to us before. We try to sort it out on the phone and in emails. We still can't figure it out. We don't talk again for several years. I have lost one of my closest and dearest friends.

I am heartbroken.

FOURTEEN

Summer 2003

The summer goes on. Nate continues to live on Lopez. After the gun incident, I distance myself from him even more.

I'm exhausted and can no longer organize my life around Nate and his addiction. I can't handle the disappointment; the pain. In fact, I start reorganizing my life *away* from Nate and his addiction. There is now an invisible wall between us. It may not be right, but it's all I can do.

Larry and I have bought a piece of property on Demeter Island. It's been a dream of Larry's since he had to sell his house there fifteen years ago. It's now a dream of mine, too and we start venturing to Demeter on weekends in our twelve- foot Boston Whaler. We camp on our little piece of property near the bay. It is south facing with sun shining all day on the beach. We have an intimate view of the point and other outer islands. We can see Orcas and San Juan Island in the distance.

The beach is a mixture of sand and gravel. There is plenty of driftwood for making forts, rafts, and back rests. When the tide comes in on the hot sandy beach the water warms up and we swim. There is a hundred-foot path through the marsh that leads to the woods where we will build a cabin. I can relax here on Demeter. We don't have a phone or internet and we only see people if we go looking for them. In the beginning we just stay there and occasionally walk down to visit Derek and Susan.

I am thoroughly in love with our little piece of beach, marsh, and woods on Demeter. It's the one place that I am free of my role as mother of an addict and as a psychotherapist.

It becomes my comfort.

It becomes my escape.

One night I get a call from the San Juan County sheriff.

Nate has been in a car accident. He is in a medical helicopter on his way from Lopez to Saint Joe's Hospital in Bellingham. He was driving. They tell me he was extremely combative with the EMTs. They say they think he was under the influence of something, but he did not have alcohol in his system. I call the hospital and they tell me they are doing a full toxicology screen. They don't give me any other information except he is not in critical condition. I call his dad and ask him to deal with it. I am emotionally exhausted and angry.

I can't deal with it.
It's the first time I have not gone to him.
I am numb.

I think that he will die from his addiction.
I can't save him.
I stay home.

I take care of Vida.
I go to Eagle Cove the next day.
I don't want to talk about it.

Vida runs naked on the beach.
We dig in the sand.
We build sandcastles.

The teenagers come with their beer and cigarettes.
We hike up the path and go home.
She takes her nap.
I nap, too.

I can't take much more of this, of him, of addiction.

I make a small altar on our large farmhouse table. Our friend Roger made it for us when we first moved into the yurts. I wanted there to be room for everyone at our table. I light a candle for Nate and place my favorite photo of him from the desert onto the alter. I find the Tibetan Buddhist mala he wore there and add it to the altar. I keep the candle lit day and night and pray that Nate will stay alive.

I say the Serenity Prayer.

God, grant me the serenity

To accept the things I cannot change,

Courage to change the things I can,

And the wisdom to know the difference.

I breathe.

The next time I talk to Nate we don't even talk about the accident. I don't want to hear about it.

I know he was on something.

I know he almost died.

I know there will be no legal consequences.

I ask him to please be careful.

I ask him to please choose life.

He cries.

I cry.

He tells me he will try.

I run into the woman in town who owns the house on Lopez that Nate is renting. She tells me how horrible things are with Nate and his friend at the house. She tells me the police are there all the time. The house is dirty and they don't take care of it. She tells me she hears they have parties and the neighbors want them to leave. She tells me there are underage girls there.

I feel sick.

I want to throw up.

I hate this.

I hate him.

They also owe her money. I am humiliated and embarrassed, yet I know it's not my fault, nor my responsibility. I see how angry she is at me, at him, at the other boy.

I feel horrible.

I understand.

I tell her I am sorry and that I have no power to make him do anything different. I tell her I will try anyway.

Now, I see her everywhere.

FIFTEEN

February 1970

The Weatherman Organization required that couples separate when they joined the Collective. Having emotional attachments to anyone could interfere with the political work. My mom was put in the Oakland Collective. My Dad was put in the San Francisco Collective. I was put in San Francisco at Bob and Barbara's house with Huey on Bocano Street. Huey was only six months old and his dad, Joe, came back to pick him up in a matter of days.

The collectives were strict with their rules. Huey's mom René was put in Oakland with my mom. They became intimate. As mothers having just abandoned their babies, they became a source of comfort for one another.

My mom was kicked out of the collective for a week when she wouldn't follow the rules. She wasn't a good enough soldier, or it may have been because she was developing an intimate relationship with Rene'.

When my mom came back to the collective, she continued her political missions. She climbed up into the hills with others from the collective for shooting practice with her grandfather's rifle and shotgun. My dad was doing the same things within his collective. There were more demonstrations, trials, planned riots, etc.

In the middle of March a townhouse was blown up on the East Coast and the Weatherman Organization was implicated in the bombing. Several members escaped, but some were killed in the bombing, including one of the recruiters my parents had met in San Leandro months before. My parents were beginning to realize the seriousness of the organization.

After the bombing the official name changed from the

Weatherman Organization to the Weather Underground. The members began bleaching their hair in efforts to disguise themselves. It was a color that became known as "weatherman orange." They were heading deeper underground.

My mom was sent out on secret missions. One day she was in the Haight on a secret mission and walked into a little boutique with all sorts of beads, necklaces, earrings, sparkly pants, leather vests, and sequined dresses. Janis Joplin was in the shop, obviously friends with the owner. Janis was known for her beads, sequins, and fringe. Everything in the store was just her style. My mom recognized Janis and hung out for a while, casually conversing about the beads, necklaces, and hippy garments. Although my mom was a fan and admired Janis greatly, she was never the type to bring someone's status into the light.

My mom had her first secret visit with me about two weeks after joining the collective. Barbara brought me to a park to meet her. My mom pushed me on the swings, hoping she would not be reported. We laughed and played together. She doesn't remember a lot about that visit. It was very strange for her. It was even stranger for me.

I cried as I watched her go. I have relived that scene in my mind a thousand times. I have relived the feeling of being left a thousand more. I stood by the empty swings, tears streaming down my freckled cheeks, reaching out for my mom. I tried so hard to get her to stay, but that did not matter, she was leaving me anyway.

I could hardly breathe.

SIXTEEN
August 2003

Nate moves home at the end of August. He stays with us in the new house. After talking to his dad and burning so many bridges on Lopez and San Juan, he has decided to try fishing on a processor boat with his dad in Alaska. They will leave in early September. He needs me to drive him to Ballard for orientation and to get his paperwork turned in so he is eligible to work on the boat.

It's a busy couple of weeks. I work, I take care of Vida, and I navigate Nate's comings and goings late into the night. He brings people to the house who I am not comfortable with. I am tense all the time. I am edgy. I tell him and his friends to leave. I tell Nate these friends are not welcome here. I don't want these friends around Vida or me.

I cook for him.

I clean up after him.

I resent him.

I resent his addictions.

It's not like the drugs and alcohol are in my face, it's just the behavior that accompanies them. It's the staying up late and sleeping in. The avoidance of responsibility and account-ability. It's the laziness and disrespect and lack of concern for others. It's the people. It's the people involved I hate the most. I know I shouldn't, but I do. They are easy to hate.

He is still my son.

He is still alive.

I still have hope.

I lie to myself. I pretend fishing will be okay, maybe even good for Nate, though I know the fishing industry is fraught with drugs and alcohol. Nate has had very little time with his dad, sometimes not seeing him for months at a time and then only for a day or if he's lucky, a weekend.

He needs to know his dad. He needs to get out of Friday Harbor. He needs to work. Fishing with Glen will give him these opportunities. He will be working hard and he should be sober while he's on the boat. I have no control over any of it.

I let go.

I breathe.

I say the Serenity Prayer.

God, grant me the serenity
To accept the things I cannot change,
Courage to change the things I can,
And the wisdom to know the difference.

Again.

And again.

He will leave in five days.

It's Friday night, September twelfth. Nate has been at the house for a couple of weeks and despite the bits of underlying tension, we are getting along.

It's been one of those beautiful September days in the San Juan's. Early morning fog burning off by noon, clear blue skies, and warm. We look forward to our Indian summers. Vida and I have spent our morning and early afternoon savoring it all at Eagle Cove.

Nate sleeps half the day away in his new room, which he has finally painted a very bright blue. I can't stand the color or the job he did. But I am still attempting to get Nate to take ownership of his room and the new house. I want so badly for him to feel welcomed and loved in the new house and in the new configuration of our family since Vida's arrival. He can be very sweet with Vida. He is going through the motions for me. He doesn't want to hurt me and I am trying hard not to feel hurt.

Tonight Nate is home. He eats the quesadillas that I make for dinner. I put Vida to bed around seven-thirty and Nate asks me if I can give him a ride to town. I begrudgingly drive him the two miles to town and drop him at the Little Store. I hate it when he goes out. I hate being any part of it. I worry the whole night that he will die or I will get a call from the sheriff that he has been arrested. I worry about dealing with a drunk, loud Nate at two in the morning, making food and disrupting our peaceful house. The whole time he is out I feel sick, and can't sleep.

I get home five minutes after dropping him off and the sun has just set. I look out the front windows at the horizon and see emergency lights. I hear sirens, a lot of sirens. It looks like the lights are on Bailer Hill Road, between us and False Bay. It's slightly dark and getting darker, so the emergency lights are bright. I point the lights out to Larry and I think it must be a car accident. Since I have just dropped Nate off minutes before, I am not worried that he's involved. I get ready for bed.

The phone rings.

"Hi Mom, can you come get me?" Nate says.

"Yes," I say.

"I am still at the Little Store," he says.
"There has been an accident."
"Millhouse was hit by a car," he tells me.
"Everyone is going home."
"No one is out."

"Oh, no."
"I will be right there," I say.

I throw on some shorts and flip-flops and drive back down Lampard Road, onto Spring Street, and he's right there waiting for me in front of the Little Store. He hops in the car. He is visibly shaken. Ryan with his big black afro, also known as Millhouse, had been Nate's friend since kindergarten. Not best friends, but good friends. They have spent hours and hours together as boys and young men. Once he and Ryan thought it would be a good idea to make a little fire on the yurt deck after school. They almost burned the house down. For years there was a burnt spot on the yurt deck where they tried their little experiment.

Nate tells me Ryan is being flown off-island in a medical helicopter. He was riding his bike home after working at Kings Market. A car hit him. He thinks the people who hit him might also be friends of his. My heart breaks for Ryan's mom, Toni. Ryan's dad died just months earlier from a long battle with cancer. I adore Toni. She works at the elementary school. She is one of those moms who has always been kind to Nate and me.

I know Ryan was riding his bike because he got a DUI. He was finishing his probation and was supposed to leave for film school in California in a week or two. My heart aches. I see Nate's heart is aching too. We are both fearing for Ryan's life. The little bits of information Nate can get from friends and from the online newspaper don't sound hopeful.

After talking for a few minutes he goes back into his room and watches TV. I go into my room and lay down. From my bed I can see out the living room window Bailer Hill on the horizon; the emergency lights are still flashing. It's been an hour since I heard the helicopter leave with Ryan for Harborview in Seattle. I lay in my bed watching the lights, thinking about Toni and praying for Ryan's life, knowing it just as easily could have been Nate. I can't make sense of it.

I barely breathe.

SEVENTEEN

March 1970

My mom was still absent.
She was still underground.

I missed her.

I lived with Bob and Barbara in San Francisco for three long weeks before my dad showed up one day to take me home. He had been kicked out of the Weather Underground Collective in San Francisco because he was argumentative and couldn't get along with the other radicals. The final conflict was something about a stereo. Maybe it was his stereo. He took the stereo and left.

My dad and I stayed with a friend in Berkeley. He was going to hang out with me and try and figure out what to do next. He was relieved to be out of the tense and volatile collective. He was reconnecting with old friends and acquaintances and he took me with him wherever he went.

We were a pair.

My dad made friends with a woman named Libby. She had three children, Christopher, Jennifer, and Thomas, who was my age. We all hung out at the park and Libby's house for weeks. Libby's husband and she were separated at the time, making her a single mom of three, with a baby on the way. Libby had big, loopy brown curls and large, intense eyes. She was an artist and a hippie just like us.

My dad took me to Winchel's in the mornings to get boxes of donuts, coffee for him, milk for me and then we were off to the park's annex to hang out for the day. My dad smoked a lot of pot while he was hanging out with me at the park. It was our morning routine and we met Libby and her children there, too.

My mom soon found out my dad had picked me up, but I don't think she knew about Libby. She found a secret way to communicate with him and arranged a visit with me at the park annex. I was happy to see my mom, to swing and play with her, but I was devastated, and crying when she left me, again. I cried even harder than the time before. I was more confused because she was leaving me and my dad.

I had no idea why she kept leaving me.

I had no idea how to get her to stay.

Being away from me, encountering the militant direction of the Weather Underground and the traumatic visits with me in the park finally infiltrated my mom's mind. She was starting to come back to her senses, returning to the reality of being my mom. She wanted to be my mom more than she wanted to stop the war in Vietnam.

She told René and her friend Leslie that she wanted out. They weren't too keen on letting my mom out of the organization. Leslie was in the San Francisco collective and was a good and trusted soldier for the movement.

She was higher in the ranks and had more power than my mom. Leslie, knowing my mom as well as she did from the early days in Seattle, and knowing how much my mom loved me, used her influence and negotiated my mom's release. As soon as my mom was allowed to leave, she found my dad and me hanging out in Oakland.

Finally, we were back together. My parents rented a little apartment in Berkeley. René and Huey were living with us. My parents didn't have jobs yet and were living off food stamps. They took turns selling the progressive alternative newspaper on the street corner for a bit of extra change.

My mom was a night owl, so she took the night shift after I had fallen asleep. She wore her blue jeans, tall black high-heeled leather boots, and her purple suede jacket with fringe hanging from the sleeves. She walked the streets late at night talking with people about politics and trying to convince them to buy the paper.

In Berkeley my mom connected with Country Joe McDonald personally and his daughter Seven, who was my age. My mom got involved in helping start a little alternative preschool on Bateman Street in Berkeley. The preschool was Tom Hayden and Ann Wiell's idea. Some of the members of the Red Family had enough money to buy a house in 1968, on Hillegas, which shared a yard with what became the Blue Fairyland Preschool.

My parents lived nearby in Oakland. On Haddon Road we lived with Bob Sabatini. Bob was openly gay and an artist. He painted large acrylic paintings, and pennies covered the floor of his room. He was obscure, creative, and extremely talented. He looked like Guido Sarducci with his slightly balding black hair, dark eyes, and olive skin. He wore a black beret. He wore button-up blousy shirts and snug jeans. He was not really a kid person, but was quite fond of me and we hung out often at the house, me doing my thing and him doing his.

Robby came to visit us occasionally, as he was in and out of trial and had since moved back to Seattle. Robby had known me since I was a baby in the U-District. He was always teasing me, tickling me and singing me songs. His favorite and mine, was "Charlie Brown." He would sing in a very playful deep voice and I would laugh and laugh, begging him to sing it again and again.

Bob and my parents did odd jobs together to make money. They had a truck and took people's stuff to the dump and did yard work. A perk of the job was acquiring furniture from other people's dump piles around Oakland. Once there was a beveled antique mirror they found and brought home. It had small flowers and ribbons carved in the dark-brown frame with a gold patina. The mirror itself had dark streaks running through it from age. I climbed up on a chair so I could see myself in that mirror and checked out my current outfit or the braids my mom had just finished.

My parents, however, were growing weary of the city life and longed for the country, especially the laid back, down-to-earth feel of the Northwest. They had been out of the Weatherman Underground for not quite two years by now. My mom wanted to settle down in a little rural community, maybe have a small farm with a garden, chickens, pigs, and a horse for me.

Robby had been going back and forth between Seattle, where he was in law school again at the University of Washington, and Oakland where he had legal issues. He had some friends that had been living on a little farm on Whidbey Island. They were moving and the little farmhouse was up for rent. My mom knew immediately she wanted to live there. They took the house sight unseen and packed up the VW bus again, then we headed north on I-5 to Washington.

My parents had found their way back to that little island that they had driven down once when I was just a newborn. The little farmhouse on Whidbey Island was just five miles from the Clinton ferry. It was a blue house with white trim, right across from the elementary school where I was going to attend kindergarten in September.

It was a cold, dark, and rainy February and my mom had just conceived my brother. The house was on twenty-six acres of beautiful open pasture, with apple and cherry trees spread throughout. We had a big red barn with a rope swing hanging from the rafters and hay piled high to land in.

Behind our farm was an even larger piece of property that had a huge wooded area and huge untouched meadows. In the spring there were large rings of little white mushrooms; my mom called them fairy rings. There were also patches of mint that we picked to make tea.

Our property was known as Raspberry Flats and the

property behind us was called Fairyland because of those fairy rings and the hippies who lived there. Everything about that farm and Fairyland was magic to me. The woods, the meadows, the flowers, and the people.

There were several families living in Fairyland in rundown outbuildings turned into little cabins with funky wood stoves. There were many hippies who were new to Whidbey that simply camped out in Fairyland until they could find housing.

There were children to play with and usually some unemployed hippie singing or playing guitar. Everyone seemed happy and relaxed, perhaps because they were smoking a lot of pot, drinking, maybe taking mushrooms or other psychedelics, but as a little girl I was oblivious to it all. Everyone was mellow. There were plenty of latenight bonfires and trails to walk through on dark nights.

My mom painted my room lavender because it was my favorite and it was the color I chose. My mom always let me choose those sorts of things. She believed in giving me freedom. My room was in the back of the small farmhouse and had a teeny little door that only I could walk through without bending over.

My mom sewed curtains for the window above the sink and for the windows in the nook where she put the kitchen table. I ran in and out of that kitchen a thousand times, banging the door behind me every time. Living in the country was a new kind of freedom.

The living room was small, but open to the kitchen. My dad built me a rustic, very funky, little desk from old grey plywood and a bench at the living room window, so I could sit and look out while I was drawing the scenes of the meadow and apple orchard outside.

My mom wanted a garden, so she and my dad spent the spring preparing the soil and planting seeds. By summer her pregnant belly was starting to push out of her intricately embroidered overalls. Her garden was abundant with carrots, lettuce, peas, radishes, spinach, and tons of broccoli.

That summer I ran barefoot in and out of the garden all day long. I eagerly helped water, weed, and harvest the garden. We had chickens and I traipsed out in the early mornings to feed them their chicken scratch in my yellow flannel nightgown.

With my little five-year-old hands I took scoops from the bucket and threw the scratch to the little clutch of hens and their one rooster. He was the biggest and crowed fervently every morning, but I was not afraid. I looked for their eggs and gathered the ones I found hidden in the little hay nests on their roosts. The eggs were caramel colored and warm. I was so careful, carrying them gently in my little basket and delivering them to my mom in the kitchen.

One morning I went to the barn early and was feeding the chickens when that rooster came at me. He was screeching, biting, flapping his black shimmering wings and clawing at me. He was even pecking at me with his sharp beak and I was frozen in terror. I was powerless to stop him.

I was screaming and crying when my mom came flying out of the house in her flannel nightgown. She scooped me up in her arms.

Later that day my dad put the rooster on the chopping block and with his axe took the head right off. It ran around the yard for a while with his head chopped off and blood dripping down its feathers, which was almost as scary as being attacked. Finally he laid down and died.

I felt relieved.

I felt protected.

I felt safe.

I breathed.

EIGHTEEN

September 2003

Ryan is dead.

Nate is sleeping.

I imagine how Nate will feel. I wonder how he'll process Ryan's death. He is leaving for Alaska in a few days. He is eighteen years old. He will be on a huge processor boat in Alaska with twenty men he doesn't know. He will have his dad, but they aren't close. How can I send my son off to Alaska on a fishing boat for two months just days after losing one of his close friends?

When Nate wakes up he already knows. A friend has called. He knows more about what happened to Ryan than I do, and we both learn more as the days progress.

Ryan was riding his bike home after work. He was a mile from home. He passed his mom just minutes before on Douglas Road. She was headed to the China Pearl for dinner with her friends, Jill and Jennifer, and slowed down to say hi to him.

"I thought we were having dinner together," he says.

"Mom, if you're not going to be home maybe I'll stay out!"

"Oh no, you get on home, big boy!"

"I'll see you later. I love you," she says.

"I love you, too," Ryan says as he rides home.

The young woman driving doesn't see Ryan when she drives up Bailer Hill Road that night to watch the sunset, a favorite teenage pastime, which usually involves drugs and alcohol. The sun shines in such a way and at such an angle that she cannot see him at just the wrong moment. She hits Ryan as he rides his bike up Bailer Hill, her speed and intoxication are factors. She panics, drives off, turns down a dirt road, hides her car and calls friends to pick her up. In the passenger seats are one of Ryan's best friends and two classmates.

It's awful.

No one can make sense of Ryan's death.

There is hiding.
There is lying.
There is blaming.

There is fear.
There is pain.
There is suffering.

There is hope for forgiveness.
There is hope for healing.
There is more pain.
And more pain.
And even more.

It's unbearable.

I drive Nate to the ferry the day before Ryan's memorial. I am distraught that Nate won't be able to grieve with his friends. He won't be able to grieve with me. I want him to stay home and attend the memorial. He wants to go fishing. If he doesn't go today he will lose his spot.

I can't stop him.

Vida and I drive him in my white Volvo wagon, the one I replaced the Previa with, to the ferry dock. His dad is going to pick him up in Anacortes and they will stay in Seattle tonight and fly out from Sea-Tac in the morning.

I call Glen to tell him about Ryan. Glen understands. He

feels for Nate. He has been through similar losses. He assures me he will take care of him on the boat.

I am skeptical.

It's bittersweet. I am proud he is brave enough to go on an enormous commercial fishing boat in Alaska and I am happy he will get to spend two months with his dad, doing the job his dad has been doing since he was eighteen. I am hopeful the trip will be healing.

I'm also worried. Fishing is extremely hard work. I know Nate is physically strong enough, but will he be emotionally strong enough after Ryan's death?

I take comfort in the fact he won't be in Friday Harbor around me, drinking, driving, and using drugs. I take comfort in the fact that he will be working hard. I take comfort in the fact that his life is no longer in my hands. I take comfort in the fact that he is in God's hands when he is fishing, while he is out on the Bering Sea. This is easier for me to accept. It makes it easier for me to let go.

We wait for the ferry. It's a little late and the cars are still unloading. He wears his long chino shorts, a hooded black sweatshirt and a black NY Yankees flat-bill hat, worn backwards on his shaved head. He carries his sleeping bag in one hand and his old black Tiger Football gear bag with its white strap slung across his big, strong man-body. He has a small red-and-black backpack slung on his other shoulder. He wears short white socks and black house slippers. He smiles.

Down by the ferry dock Vida is wearing her black and rainbow colored hand-knit zip-up cardigan and black leggings. Her feet are bare. Her dark brown hair is getting longer, past her shoulders, but she still has thick bangs that hang right at her eyebrows. Her brown skin is especially dark from the summer sun. She sits by Nate on the rock bench by the ice cream shop.

She keeps her hand on him as much as is possible. The last few days since Ryan died, Nate's been home more. Vida is almost three now and has spent the morning with him in her lavender footie pajamas. She lay in his bed with him watching TV and eating popcorn with butter and brewer's yeast. We both feel a little closer to him as he walks down the ramp to the ferry.

I hold Vida in my arms.

We wave goodbye.

I cry.

I breathe.

NINETEEN
Fall 1972

I woke up early on a late October morning to the sound of a baby crying. I jumped out of bed and rushed through the little doorway of my lavender room straight into my parents' bedroom. I found my mom lying on the bed with a chubby baby cradled in her arms. My dad, Robby and the midwife by her side.

I was giddy with excitement and pride for my new baby brother. I had been waiting for him. He was a chunky and a healthy eight pounds, fifteen ounces. My parents took a month to name him, deciding, finally, on Oliver.

I brought him to my afternoon kindergarten class for show-and-tell as soon as my mom let me. I carried him across the street to school. My mom was right beside me, but I felt like I was alone. I felt like I was doing it myself. I felt like he was my baby.

I was in love.

My life on Whidbey was idyllic. Later, I found out there were issues between my parents. My parents' friend Libby had been living in Seattle for a while with her four kids, and my dad and she were continuing a romantic relationship. My mom knew about it. She tried to be open and progressive about it, since it was the seventies, but she didn't like it.

Occasionally, my dad would go into the city and spend time with Libby and her children. Sometimes he took me with him. Other times, our whole family drove the VW bus into Seattle and stayed in the city with Libby and her four kids for a weekend. Libby and her children came periodically to Whidbey and stayed with us, too. We children played for hours, oblivious to the complexity of adult relationships.

I loved playing with Jennifer, who I looked up to and was Libby's only girl. Thomas was my age and we were the closest. As much as my mom loved Libby, these were painful times. She did her best to protect me from her pain.

But she could not protect me.

A daughter feels her mother's pain.

The mother carefully tucks it deep inside.

But the daughter feels it anyway.

TWENTY

Winter 2003

I'm nervous to see Nate. What will he be like after his first sixty days fishing? What will he be like two months after Ryan has died?

When he walks down the dock to us, I know instantly nothing is different. He has little to say. He is defensive. He is exhausted after working a minimum of sixteen hours a day for sixty days. He needs me to drive him to Ballard to the company office to pickup his paycheck. The check is not as big as he had hoped. He still wants to buy clothes. I take him to the Alderwood Mall.

I drive him other places, too. He doesn't have his own car. I won't let him drive mine after totaling my Previa last year. While I drive him places he tells me he likes fishing.

"You can spit."

"You can swear," he says.

"And nobody asks you how you feel."

"I'm going back in January."

"Okay, I say.

"How was your dad?"

"Did you talk?" I ask.

"He was good."

"We talked a little."

"We played cards," he says.

"How did it feel?"

"Fine," he says.

He doesn't really want to answer my questions. I don't

blame him. I don't really know what else to do but ask questions, even though I know I should just be quiet. I ask him about drinking and using drugs on the boat.

He says he doesn't.

He says nobody does.

He says you can't.

I want to believe him.

As soon as he can, he finds a tattoo parlor and has a tattoo put on his forearm. It's big and it says MILLHOUSE. This was Ryan's nickname.

He comes and goes from the house and from his bright blue room. He comes and goes from the hall bathroom. It's dark orange with a deep red ceiling. I find empty, plastic Bic pen tubes in the bathroom drawer. Sometimes they have bitter white powder on them.

He comes in late at night. At one, two, three in the morning. I hear cars pull in and drop him off. The next day he'll sleep until one, two, three in the afternoon. I see and hear the cars drive in and out of the driveway later in the evening. They pick him up.

When they do come in the house I'm cold. I want them to leave. I don't want these people in my house. Even though I know them and I have watched them grow up in this small town, I don't like them. I used to care about some of them; now I hate them. I don't trust them with my boy. I blame them for his addiction.

They invited him into their drug world. They are the lost boys. They don't have dads. Nate tells me these boys understand him. They understand what it's like being a boy, a man, without a dad. It breaks my heart. I thought I had fixed that by marrying Larry, a man of integrity, a stable father. I thought I fixed that by letting him visit his dad, despite his dad's addictions and imperfections.

I hate Larry.

I hate Glen.

I hate my dad.

I hate myself.

The lost boys want Nate. Nate is big. Nate is strong. He is intimidating. He can help protect them. He can help them sell drugs. He can help them buy drugs. Now that he is fishing he has cash, lots of cash. They use him. He probably uses them, too.

I am still hopeful, not because I see signs of hope, but because I am a therapist and I know people can change. I believe that deep inside my son is more than a drug addict. I know he has a kind heart. I know he is not these things that drugs turn him into.

Nate changes his last name from mine to his dad's. He says it's easier for fishing. I try not to feel hurt. For Christmas I give him a huge, orange, canvas duffle bag from Lands' End, with his new name embroidered on it in white lettering. In January he takes his huge, orange, duffle bag and goes fishing, again.

He calls from the boat when he needs things. He calls for warm socks. He calls for long underwear. He calls when he loses his ID at the airport. I mail him boxes of the things he needs. I throw in Red Vines, cookies, and notes. I run around making copies and fax his ID to the airport in Dutch Harbor.

He comes home, again.

He sleeps in the bright blue room. He uses the hall bathroom, and I find rolled-up dollar bills in the bathroom drawer. Again, I find bitter white dust on the empty, plastic, Bic pen tubes. I know it's bitter because I taste it.

Nate smokes cigarettes outside by the huge, rusty metal funnel from the old gravel pit at Jackson's Beach. It has become our fire pit. He chews tobacco and leaves spit cans and bottles everywhere. He wants me to make him quesadillas. I make them. Sometimes it feels good to make my boy a quesadilla, and there is a false sense of closeness. Most of the time

I resent it. I resent him. I resent the mess he leaves every day, everywhere. I resent the constant coming and going. I think about that line in *Napoleon Dynamite* that the grandma says, "make your own damn quesadilla." I imagine saying that to him more times than I can count.

He comes home at one, two, three in the morning. I hear the cars pull in and drop him off. The next day he sleeps until one, two, three in the afternoon. I see and hear the cars drive in and out of the driveway later in the evening. They pick him up. Whoever they are, they rarely come in. When they do come in I want them to leave again.

The lost girls start showing up at my house, too. They are fifteen, sixteen, and seventeen. I know who they are. They have hard lives. They use drugs, they drink, they hang out with older guys. Nate is one of those older guys.

Only they and I know this. I worry about them. They know I am worried. I say nothing. I am kind. I am detached. I don't want them at my house. I care about them. My heart aches the whole time. I want to protect them, too.

I can't.

I can't protect anyone.

I do not want any part of this drug culture. I do not want any of it in my house or in my driveway. I want all of them to go away. I want them to leave my son alone. I want them to stop. I want him to stop.

I hate it.

I hate him.

I hate the lost boys.

I hate the lost girls.

This can't be my life.

I hate it.

I feel sick.

I grind my teeth.

I try to breathe.
I can't breathe.

I trust no one.
I trust nothing.
I don't even trust myself.
Nate talks me into driving him off-island to a car dealer. We take the 8:00 a.m. ferry to Anacortes and drive to Burlington. He has five thousand dollars for a down payment. If I cosign he can get his own car.
I know I shouldn't.
I know it's fucked up.
But I am still naive.
So, I don't know how fucked up it really is.
I am enabling him.
I am supporting his addiction.

I pretend helping him buy a car is normal.
It's what normal moms do.
I know it's not.
Not under these circumstances.
Not amid addiction.
It's not healthy.
I keep pretending.
I cosign on a rust-colored Nissan Xterra. It's practically new. It costs more than I have ever spent on a car. I feel a false sense of pride. My son has a fancy new car. See, things are okay. He loves it. He takes it out four-wheeling and he breaks it the first week. It costs thousands to fix it. He's out of control.
He can't stand me.
I can't stand him.
He has to leave.
I feel trapped in my own house. When he is not in Alaska fishing, he is on the island. He is at my house, his house. I don't feel safe leaving my house unlocked, uninhabited. I am afraid his friends will steal from us; I wonder if he will.

Larry, Vida, and I have been taking the boat to Demeter as much as possible, when Nate is fishing and the weather is warm. Our life on Demeter is growing. We are building a cabin just a short-winding trail away from the beach. I want to spend more time on our little sliver of land.

When I am there I don't have to see people who know me as Nate's mom or as their therapist or as anyone's therapist. I have no responsibilities on Demeter and everyone is kind and gentle with me. My heart can be heavy and no one expects anything from me. Whatever I share from my heart, my kitchen, my sewing machine is welcome. Although my heart aches the whole time I am there, I still feel like I am being rocked in a strong, enveloping hammock.

Demeter is what my spirit needs.

I feel safe on Demeter.

I feel protected.

I feel less alone.

My dad smoked pot almost every day of my life until I was eighteen. My dad had his gin-and-tonics, his beer, and his pot. I appreciate that my dad is sober now. He says he quit to contribute to the health of our family, to help Nate. One day, on a bike ride out to the cemetery off Madden Lane my dad makes amends with me about his unavailability due to addiction.

I appreciate dad for this and it motivates me to stop drinking. I have stopped on and off over my life. When Nate was little I didn't drink for three years. Recently, I have used wine to take the edge off a long day or to celebrate a birthday or a dinner with friends. It has been a daily habit at times and a monthly treat at other times.

As a teenager my drinking was a dangerous behavior that left me throwing up, passing out, and in unwanted and unsafe sexual situations. I repeated that behavior from the time I was fourteen until the night I conceived Nate. I stopped drinking the day after my intuition told me I was pregnant and I could no longer tolerate the smell of cigarettes or the taste of beer.

I never wanted alcohol, drugs, and the chaos that came with using them regularly. I saw the destruction clearly. I didn't stay with Nate's dad because of his addictions. I protected myself and Nate from the damage of addiction to the best of my ability. I thought I had succeeded. But no, Nate has brought addiction right into my house. I must have done something wrong.

I have not protected him.

I am outraged at myself.

What am I doing wrong?

I wait for it to change.

I hope it is a stage.

It's not.

It's getting worse.

It's not a stage.

It's addiction.

He continues coming home drunk in the middle of the night. I am still finding the remnants of cocaine in the dark orange bathroom with the dark red ceiling. The chaos of his addiction is becoming the norm of our life. He makes food in the middle of the night. It wakes Larry and me. He leaves his dishes in the sink. His room is a mess. He sleeps too much. He stays up too late. He seems angry all the time.

I feel used.

I feel angry.

I feel sick.

Since I have quit drinking I can't tolerate these feelings. I can't tolerate that coping with Nate's addiction has become my whole life. Addiction is running my life. Addiction is ruining my life. I tiptoe around it, but it's true.

I call a man I know who is in Al-Anon, and AA. I sit in his living room and tell him everything. He listens. He encourages me go to meetings. I have clients at those meetings. How can I go and talk freely and openly about how addiction is affecting me and my family if my clients were in a meeting. It crosses a therapeutic boundary. It would be unethical.

I can't go to those meetings. I need those meetings. He talks about isolation and how it keeps addiction alive. He talks about the Twelve Steps and my higher power. He talks about self-care.

I listen.

I understand.

I am enabling Nate.

I have to stop.

I need to set better boundaries. I need to stop feeling responsible for Nate's addiction. I need to let go on a whole other level. I thought I had let go enough, but I haven't. I need Al-Anon. I develop a network of people in Al-Anon that I can call to get support. I read *The Language of Letting Go* by Melanie Beattie, all day, every day. I read until I am able to let go, just a little bit more.

I can at least ask Nate to leave the house. I tell myself it's no longer my job to keep Nate alive. It's no longer my job to heal his wounds. He has to heal himself. Anything that reeks of addiction, I do not want in my house or in my life. The only place I am willing to deal with it is within myself and with my clients. Everyone else is on their own.

Larry does not understand. Larry does what I ask him to do. Larry gardens and watches Vida when I work. Larry says very little to Nate. When Larry voices his opinion, I never agree. He wants to make rules together, but I can't coparent Nate with him. His rules don't make sense to me. He wants me to do less, but I can't imagine doing less of anything right now, except less worrying. It only makes me angrier when he speaks. I can barely hear him. It's as if he is speaking a different language. I don't understand him and he doesn't understand me. He just doesn't understand addiction. I don't think he has even attempted to educate himself on the disease. I feel frustrated, disappointed and alone.

Nate sleeps all day. He wakes up, showers, dresses, and gets ready to leave in his Xterra. He is never available to talk to me. He is always leaving, busy, dismissive.

I finally catch him backing down the driveway. I stop him. He won't get out of the car. I stand in front of the car. I am angry. My body is tight. My heart is beating fast. My voice is loud. My voice is firm. I am not screaming. I am serious. I am strong.

"NATE."

"STOP," I say.

"NATE."

"I NEED TO TALK TO YOU."

"I'm going to Canada for the weekend."

"I can't talk." He dismisses me.

"I have to go."

"NATE."

"STOP," I say again.

"YOU HAVE TO TALK TO ME."

"YOU CAN'T LIVE HERE."

"YOU HAVE TO MOVE."

He keeps backing up. In his eyes I see pain. I see the same pain as when I sent him away to Anasazi. He feels betrayed. He also knows I am right. He knows he's using me. It's easier for him to live here in between fishing trips. Living with friends or getting his own place is more complicated, more expensive, riskier. I stand in front of the car. He won't get out and talk to me. The car is running. He keeps backing up.

"NATE," I say loudly,

"YOU NEED TO PACK YOUR THINGS."

"IF YOU DON'T, I WILL."

"YOU CAN'T LIVE HERE."

"IT'S NOT HEALTHY."
"YOU HAVE TO MOVE."
"Fuck," he says.
"God, Mom."
"Fine."
"I'll leave."
"When I get back from Canada, I'll pack."

I am skeptical.

"Okay."
"Thanks," I say.
"If not, I WILL pack your things."
"No matter what."
"I'm sorry."
"I love you."

"Bye," he says as he abruptly throws the Xterra in reverse.

"Bye, Nate."

The lost girls come home with Nate a few days later. They help him pack. I watch as the lost girls carry boxes from his room to his car through the kitchen and dining room, out across the lawn to where he has parked.
I feel embarrassed.
I feel humiliated.
I feel like a failure.

I detach.
I compartmentalize.
I say the Serenity Prayer.

I let go a little more.
My whole body aches as he drives away with the lost girls and his boxes.

I lay down on his bed and stare at the white ceiling.

I am dying inside.

I want to give up.

I want to throw up.

I remember what Robin told me. As long as Nate is alive there is hope. I hold onto Robin's words. I remember Toni telling the story at Ryan's memorial about how she sent Ryan home that night because he had been in trouble. He wanted to go to dinner with her, but she did the "right thing," she sent him home because he had chores. It was the right thing. But it didn't turn out right at all. It didn't keep him alive.

Tears stream down my cheeks. I think of those brave mothers. They were the mothers whose sons were gone. They did everything they could to love and protect their boys, and they couldn't. They couldn't keep them alive.

I need to find a way to let Nate go and love him despite his choices, despite his addictions, despite the pain it has caused. I have to remember the pain he is in. I have to remember that I have no control over the outcome of his life. I have to keep preparing myself to lose him.

He doesn't talk to me for months, until he loses his ID, again. Again, I fax it to the Dutch Harbor Airport. This happens repeatedly.

It's Christmas and Larry's older kids are here. I fill stockings for four adult children and Vida. I make Christmas Eve dinner and wonder if Nate will show up. He calls and says he will come tomorrow.

I hate that Larry's kids are here when my own son isn't. I rationalize and make excuses as to why Nate isn't coming. I know it's the addiction. I assume everyone else knows that, too.

I feel sick.

I go through the motions.

I compartmentalize.

I want to throw up.

I breathe.
I say the Serenity Prayer.
I focus on the good.
I focus on Vida.
Vida is good.
She is already three. She loves everything about Christmas. She loves baking and decorating star-shaped shortbread cookies. She has endless patience with any red or green glittery craft. She loves going to the San Juan Historical Museum to sit on Santa's lap, drink apple cider, sing Christmas carols, and run around outside in the dark with the other children while chestnuts roast on the fire.

I love Christmas. I love creating the magic of Santa. My mom always took the magic seriously. I want everything to feel special and magical for Vida, like it did for me. When Nate was little I created the magic for him, too.

I wrap everything just so, with real satin ribbons and expensive paper or sometimes grocery bags for a more organic look. I want everything to coordinate and I get uptight when it doesn't. Nobody in my house appreciates this obsession, but I'm committed anyway. I like to pick a winter bouquet for the table with fir, pine, and something with red berries or snow berries, if I can find them. I light fragrant candles.

After dinner, I read Vida as many Christmas books from our pile as she wants. I love the Jan Brett Christmas books best. We read *The Sweet Smells of Christmas*, from my childhood. It's a scratch-and-sniff book that my Auntie Barb had given me, but the smell faded after a while. I order a new one so Vida can smell it, too.

Finally, Vida and I finish with *The Donkey's Dream* written and illustrated by Barbara Berger. My mom gave it to me on Nate's first Christmas. It's the story of Jesus' birth from the donkey's perspective. The illustrations are dreamy watercolors and I love the prose as Mary rides with her pregnant belly on the donkey's back to Bethlehem.

After we read, I rub her back and sing all our songs, starting with "Buenos Noches Vida" to the tune of "Frére Jacques" and continuing with Favorite Things from the *Sound of Music*. I end with Malvina Reynolds, Turn Around, which my mom used to sing to me. Vida likes it best when I stay until she falls asleep.

I usually do.

It doesn't take too long. She is a good sleeper. Nate used to always fight sleep. When he was tired, he would get more hyper. Sleep was always a power struggle between us. I think he was just a natural night owl, and as a young single mom I needed him so desperately to go to sleep. It was a bad combination. Nate is the child who humbles me. He tests me. He teaches me what I need to learn. I am a slow learner. I do my best. I could do better.

While Vida sleeps, I fill her stocking with barrettes, little stuffed animals, art supplies, red and green M&M's, a clementine, a big candy cane and, as always, a toothbrush.

I leave the Christmas tree lights on all night. I go to bed. I toss and turn, anxious about tomorrow. Will Nate show up? I have only gotten him one present. It is a t-shirt from the thrift store, tags still on it; it's dark green and says, "bah humbug" in red. I know this will not feel good to him. But it's the truth. It's how I feel about him and his addictions. I don't feel like giving him anything.

He shows up early Christmas morning. He is pasty white and blotchy, his eyes half closed. Perhaps he is on something. I have no idea. He isn't really with us. He has brought no presents. He brings no joy.

I pretend it's normal.

We all know it isn't.

I feel sick.

I wait for it to be over.

I wait for him to leave.

I grind my teeth.

My body hurts.

I can barely breathe.

I do my best to stay calm on the outside as we open presents and have breakfast while Larry and his kids make conversation with Nate about fishing. Nate tells big stories about the size of fish, the size of the waves, and the size of his paycheck. I listen. I try to care, but all I can think about is what I have learned to call, in my mind, the red stamp of addiction. It's what I put on everything that reeks of, or is caused by, addiction.

I stop caring about the stories.

It's too painful.

I'm too exhausted.

I long for the day to be over. I wait for Nate to say he has to leave. I wait for him to say he needs a ride to the ferry. He wants to leave, too. These visits are not easy for him either. At four o'clock I take him to the ferry. Our goodbye is stiff and unemotional. We no longer have anything to say to each other. He sees the pain in my eyes. I see the pain in his, too. Neither of us can do anything about it.

"Bye Nate," I say,

"Take care of yourself."

"Bye Mom."

"I will," he says.

I don't believe him.

He gets out of the car and walks to a car in the ferry line. I turn my eyes away and drive slowly up an empty Spring Street. No one is in town on Christmas Day. Everyone is at home with their families.

On my way home, I pull over for a moment and sit, dreading the conversation that will ensue about Nate with Larry and his kids, but mostly we will be silent. There is nothing too positive that can be said about Nate right now and in Larry's family they painfully avoid talking about anything negative. Anything said about Nate will be forced, and for me, unbearable.

The unraveling has begun. But I pretend it isn't. I say, it's an old sweater. It's an old relationship. It just has a loose thread, a little, bitty hole. It's not a problem. I am just stressed. It's normal, I tell myself. I know it's a problem. I just don't know how big a problem it is. I can still disguise it.

I take a deep breath.

I turn into my driveway.

Once inside, I curl up on the couch and read another pile of Christmas books with Vida. We organize and put away all her new presents. She has a mound of clothes, books, and toys from friends and family. We make a special place in her room and play area for each gift.

I tuck her into her colorful horse sheets from Garnet Hill, her citron-green comforter and the purple velvet quilt I made before she was born. I lay my tired body next to hers and rub her back.

I sing.

I survive Christmas.
Barely.

I breathe.

TWENTY-ONE

Winter 2005

Vida is four, and it's been a year and a half since I demanded Nate move out. Life has been calmer, but Vida has been more challenging. Although she is sweet, compliant, helpful, happy, and kind most of the time, we have difficult moments. She is so good so much of the time that eventually she just snaps and can no longer regulate her emotions or her behavior for one more minute.

There are many layers to the reasons for her behavior. Some of it is related to attachment and bonding. She is afraid of being left. She is afraid of being out of control. She is insecure about her attachment to me and her relationships with others.

Luisa gave her up when she was only two days old. She lost her foster mom when she was five months old. I am her third mother. She knows on a deep level she could lose me, too. I work with all her feelings in a conscious and unconscious way. I provide consistency and structure. I give her age appropriate choices. I give her power when I can. I take charge when I need to. I talk with her about her feelings and help her learn to express herself in healthy ways.

The pain I feel about Nate's addiction and his absence in all our lives affects her. Every time the phone rings I wonder if this will be the call, when I find out Nate is dead. Although I compartmentalize, I'm aware enough to know she feels it.

I'm always a little bit sad.

I'm always a little bit angry.

I'm always a little bit in pain.

When I first brought Vida home, she witnessed a lot of anger and tension between Nate and me. He was angry all the time. As much as I wanted to protect her, as much as I tried to protect her, I couldn't.

When she was a toddler, she used to bite other children. I worked with her teaching her not to bite. I taught her to say, "I feel like biting you," instead of actually biting. Eventually she stops biting. Eventually she stops feeling like biting. She learns to take time away from her friends. I learn not to take her too many places where there are children. I stop scheduling play dates days ahead of time. She can only have spontaneous play dates because she has to be in the mood. I attune to her more.

Lately, Vida has been extremely emotional and physically violent towards me. When she doesn't want to comply or cooperate she has huge tantrums, which include hitting me, or trying to hit me. She screams that she wants to go back to Guatemala. She is so angry. I am patient with her anger and her behavior.

Vida isn't fully regulating her emotions. I am not always regulating mine. I never taught Nate to regulate his. I devise a plan that will reward Vida for regulating her feelings. It usually involves reading her several books if she can calm herself. It works most of the time.

Vida and I are home alone one day as we often are. Vida has a huge tantrum; she screams at me and pushes me. I won't give her whatever it is she wants. She is demanding. She is out of control. I am calm. I pick her up. I can still hold her fairly easily. I hold her on my hip with two hands as I walk from the kitchen to the living room. Vida, with her small open hand, slaps me hard across the face.

It hurts.

I'm in shock.

Without thinking I let my hands go and drop her on the floor. She falls three feet to the ground and lands directly on her tailbone. She lets out one blood-curdling scream. I lift her up immediately and she falls limp in my arms. In that split second before dialing 911, I want to curl up and die. I shake her.

She is unconscious in my arms. Her eyes are rolled back in her head. She is limp. I reach over the kitchen-counter shelf and grab the phone and dial 911 with one hand. I tell the dispatcher I think my daughter is dead. My heart is beating faster than ever before.

What have I done?

Have I killed her?

Does she have a pulse?

Yes, she has a pulse.

Within seconds I hear sirens.

Please God, don't let her die.

I promise I'll change.

Her whole little life passes before my eyes. The paramedic, EMTs, and deputy walk in my front door. Just seconds before, Vida eyes have finally opened. She has come back to consciousness.

I haven't killed her.

She is alive.

I breathe.

I imagine the paramedics, EMTs, and deputy think I am a child abuser. I stay close, very close, to Vida the rest of the day.

I can hardly function.

I call and leave a message for Don. I need his help. Yes, it's an emergency. I can never, ever let that happen again. I can't let Vida engage me physically. I can't let her be physical with me ever again. We both have to learn how to regulate our strong emotions. I need to be able to keep holding on, even when it hurts, even when I'm angry, even when I am at the end of my rope.

I feel like my whole life is falling apart.

I feel like I am falling apart.

Don calls me back at the end of the day. I walk into the

bedroom, shut the door, sit on my bed, and talk on the phone with him for fifty minutes. He understands immediately the fear and pain I am feeling. He understands and says the words.

"You were dropped, metaphorically," he says.

"You dropped Vida."

"No one picked you up."

"You felt alone."

"What you did with Vida was different, Cere."

"You picked her up."

"You can repair your relationship with Vida."

"How, Don?"

"How can I fix this?" I say.

"You can't let her engage you like that, Cere."

"You have to stop letting her control your emotions."

"You have to teach her to regulate hers," he says firmly.

"Okay, Don."

"But how?" I ask.

We figure out what I can say and do to help Vida.

It will be hard. It won't work right away. She will pound on my door. She will try and get me to react. I have to be patient. I have to change the pattern. My mom and dad never tried to change these patterns. My dad was absent, angry, and impatient. He would threaten to hit me and he even did a few times. Mostly, though, he just yelled and bullied me. I was scared of his anger. I felt belittled. I never felt helped.

My mom was nice, all the time. She didn't understand me, but she was loving and patient. She was never able to guide me through my emotions or teach me how to regulate them. She allowed me to be mean to her and rarely with consequence. Only once, when I was fourteen, I told her to fuck off and she slapped me across the face. Other times she just shut down; pulled away. She was absent.

I don't want to drop Vida ever again, physically or emotionally. I want to be present no matter how difficult. I do not want to be absent. I do not want to hurt her. I want to lift her up.

Don helps me.
He attunes to me.

He never drops me.
It's been ten years.

I breathe.

Nate is still fishing. He is out on the Bering Sea sixty to ninety days and then home sixty to ninety days. He lives in Bellingham. I rarely see him or hear from him. He gets a DUI and calls me. I go with him to court, etc. I don't like it. I hope it helps. I don't offer to pay for a lawyer or give him money. I don't feel bad about these consequences. I am glad he got the DUI. I hope this will be the thing that motivates him to change. It doesn't.

I hate it.

I hear from him less and less. I go to the house where he lives with the other addicts. Where he lives with the other lost boys and lost girls. It's dirty. It's dark. There are pit bulls. I attempt to resign myself to the reality that this is the life he is choosing. It feels fatal, yet I have no control.

I hate it.
I feel sick.

In Friday Harbor I work Tuesday, Wednesday, and Thursday. I moved my office to a little cabin on our property. I avoid town and people in general. I am still carrying a heavy dose of shame about Nate's addiction. I still feel it's my fault. I still feel if I could only do the right thing he would stop, get better, be himself again.

On Friday's Larry, Vida, and I pack up the boat and go to

Demeter. We fill cardboard apple boxes with food, clothes, and other supplies. I fill the cooler with ice. Vida and I layer our big, warm, waterproof coats over our summer dresses and pull on leggings, wool socks, and rubber boots. We pull on our warmest hats and haul the boat to the Jackson's Beach boat ramp.

Early on we have a twelve-foot Boston Whaler. Later we have a boat Larry welded himself. It's a big landing craft, much warmer, less difficult to land on the beach and to maneuver in the water.

Our friend, Ebony, has been building our cabin all winter. It's late spring and almost finished. We are on Demeter as much as we can be. We eat at the rickety, weathered, gray, rough-cut cedar picnic table.

When we arrive on Demeter we unload our apple boxes and bags on the beach. We carry them up the trail one at a time and in the wheelbarrow.

After we get our supplies put away, Vida and I ride bikes on the dirt road and buy a box of veggies from Joel and Margaret. We strap the box to the back of my bike and ride the mile back home. The narrow dirt road is lined with tall fir and cedar trees, salal bushes, and hot pink flowering currant. Every now and then there is a dirt driveway to another house or cabin. We take our time. Sometimes a pickup truck passes us or we see someone else walking or riding their bike. Most of the time we see no one, just the filtered sun shining through the thick forest.

Settled into the cabin, I unpack the box of veggies into our larder. I've brought coffee and half-and-half in the cooler. There is nothing more satisfying than hot coffee and cream on early mornings in the woods.

I bring butter, cheese, and other staples to add to our veggies. We have a refrigerator-size larder upstairs in the kitchen and I have stores of rice, pasta, and oatmeal in there. Ebony built it. The larder is one of my favorite aspects of the kitchen. The pine is clear and Ebony has added some red trim to it. It makes cooking on Demeter simpler.

I'm in love with the vintage glass knobs on all the pine cabinets and drawers. I found them at a garage sale. Inside we have a very funky vintage wood cookstove, as well as a propane cookstove. Outside the claw-foot tub is tucked between two tall fir trees. We fill the tub with cold water from the hose. After it's full, Larry builds a fire under the tub to heat the water. Everything at our little Demeter house is rustic, a bit funky, and unique. Everything in our little cabin makes me feel something.

The outside of the house is board and batten, and stained dark brown with red window trim, clear cedar shingles, and a dark brown metal roof. It blends right into the forest. From the beach I can barely spot it through the cattails, brush-and-trees.

I am in love with this cabin.

I wash dishes in tubs outside after boiling water in a big pot. It's soothing to wash dishes outside while looking out through the marsh and over the bay towards the point.

On the woodsy part of the trail to the beach, Larry has hung a trapeze for Vida in one of the big fir trees. The trail in back leads to the outhouse. She and I paint a moon, hearts, and lots of green and orange stripes on the outhouse. She writes her name, too. I love our outhouse, as much as one can love an outhouse.

Vida is at the age of dressing up. She wears tutus, wings, and twirly skirts wherever she goes. She carries her American Girl doll, Josephina, with her brown skin and dark hair, everywhere. I sew her and Josephina matching skirts. Bishop, our black lab, follows Vida all over the property and through the muddy marsh trail to the warm beach.

Vida makes friends with two little girls that live a few trails away. Sonja, who is two months older than Vida, and Iris, who is two years younger. Their mom, Alison, and I grow close like sisters, the way mothers can. We breathe in and out together the naked intimacy of mothering daughters.

We play.
We eat.
We sing.
We dance.

We live at the beach and Cindy's pond. We talk and talk about the messiness in our houses and in our hearts. We meet at late-night parties, potlucks, and bonfires on the beach. We whip our organic cream by shaking it in a mason jar with a bit of maple syrup. Alison bakes us bread and chocolate molten baby cakes. The girls sew purses, bookmarks, and make rose-water to sell at the craft fair, at the one-room schoolhouse.

On our favorite nights we stroll a mile down the quiet dirt road to the point and play with Jessica, Thomas, Susan and Derek. Jessica, a pirate and an experienced New York and San Francisco bartender, builds a driftwood bar on the beach. Jess teaches the girls the subtle details of mixology and bartending. They serve our mojitos with homegrown mint, and Demeter Sunsets with grenadine in mason jars. We bury our toes in the sand, leaning back on the driftwood logs as we watch the sun set over Saturna Island.

The girls are inseparable. Larry joins us in the evenings, but the rest of the time he is on the property clearing brush, chopping firewood, and keeping all our off-the-grid systems running smoothly. It's the sweetest of times.

Vida and I are both free. She is free to be five and in her imagination. I am free to simply be a mother with a daughter. I can talk about Nate if I want, but I don't have to. I can take off my therapist hat on Demeter, too.

We pick blackberries, stir them into our favorite gluten-free pancake batter and pour them into the hot cast iron pan. We drench them in butter and real maple syrup, eating outside in the morning sun.

I never want to leave.

I nap.
I sing.

I read.
I sleep.
I breathe.
I stay as long as possible.

Every time.

TWENTY-TWO
1979

When we moved to Saratoga Road, I was seven. Oliver was two. I wasn't sad to leave the house on Maxwelton. With some help on the down payment from my Auntie Barb, my parents were able to buy the house on Saratoga, which meant we would never have to move again.

It was our house.

It was my house.

I loved everything about it.

I loved the circular driveway and the big fir trees that surrounded it. I loved the horse corral, the small field, and covered stalls for Ginger. I loved the little back porch that went the full length of the house and the covered front porch that led you to the front door and into the living room. I loved the little yellow outbuilding that my mom turned into a preschool for my brother and his friends. She called it the Yellow Cabin Preschool.

The main house was painted white when we first moved in. I loved the kitchen with its vintage white-enamel cook stove with a warmer up top. The half-moon shaped breakfast nook with windows that gave us a view of the circular driveway and vegetable garden.

It was on three acres. Just enough space to still have our pigs, Sexist and Racist, our chickens, and a horse. The forest and trails were deep enough to make elaborate and faraway forts amongst the salal and huckleberry bushes. The property was full of mature rhododendrons, lilacs, laurels, and a dogwood tree, whose branches would become my favorite spot to sit and contemplate.

Most of our furniture was from one of my parents' childhood homes or garage sales. The pieces were mostly dark wood with marble, and velvet upholstery.

To heat the house we had an airtight woodstove. My dad stacked the firewood on the back porch. It was our only heat for the winter. I liked to help my dad with the firewood. I put my arms out and he would load me up with three, four or five pieces of wood and I carried it in the house and stacked it by the stove. He taught me how to chop the cedar kindling into small pieces with the hatchet, too. I chopped carefully on the fir chopping block until I had a pile of kindling to carry into the house.

Once, when I was eight, my dad and I built a little trellis for the rosebush planted in the center of our circular driveway. My dad wasn't a builder or particularly good with his hands, so it was rare for us to work on a project together. We used cedar pieces nailed together and some string to help hold up that one rosebush. My dad was really there that day. It felt like the trellis was holding us up, too.

Saratoga Road marked a time of daily bike rides with gangs of neighborhood children. After school and on weekends we met on the road by someone's driveway and picked up anyone who wanted to join on the way as we rode through the streets. Most of the time we ended up at Helen's Store, where we emptied our pockets of change on the counter and left with them full of candy.

When it rained I stayed home with my mom. We baked, we drew, and made play dough with salt, flour, cream of tartar, and food coloring. We listened to "Free to Be You and Me" for hours and hours; "William's Doll," "Parents Are People," "Ladies First," "It's Alright to Cry," and "Glad to Have a Friend Like You."… they were all my favorites.

I also played for hours with my favorite doll, Judy, a Madame Alexander. She had been my mom's doll when she was a little girl. My mom turned the living room closet into a dollhouse for Judy. Each shelf in the closet was a separate room. Judy's old wicker furniture fit perfectly. My mom knit a poncho for Judy and sewed her new outfits. My favorite was a hand-stitched, little, back floral, two-piece bathing suit.

Besides Judy, I still had my horse Ginger. When I grew out of Ginger when I was ten, my parents bought me another horse, Caballo and then another, Coqueil. I never had more than one horse at a time and each one challenged me to the next level. For a few years I was in 4-H with my friends, Ursula and Chiara.

Our mothers supported our horseriding and 4-H. We practiced all spring and then entered our horses in the fair. We camped at the fairgrounds that whole hot week in August. We kept our horses in the stalls, made posters, and scooped poop. We rode in all the games—barrel racing, poles, dressage, etc.—and rode in the fair parade on Saturday through the streets of Langley. We stayed up late and ran around the fairgrounds riding the scary rides late into the night, until we went back to our tents exhausted and satisfied. The next day we did it all again, no matter how hot and dusty we were.

When we weren't riding in the fair, my mom would let Ursula and I pack our lunches and ride our horses the three miles down Lone Lake Road to Goss Lake. She drove there later and met us with my brother in tow. We tied up our horses in the shade and swam all day.

Goss Lake was a clear, deep lake and had no motor boats. The road to Goss Lake was canopied by big alders that we called a tree tunnel. Before we turned the corner we guessed how many cars would be in the parking lot. On a hot weekend day maybe seven or ten, and on weekdays, maybe three or four.

There was a long, steep dirt hill at the lake where my mom, brother, and I spent hours digging rivers that went all the way down to the water's edge. My mom was famous for them. We spent every sunny day possible at Goss Lake swimming and digging those rivers.

My dad was selling real estate in Langley for Island Properties. My mom sold concessions at the Clyde, the local theatre and ran her Yellow Cabin Preschool. As a family we occasionally road our bikes the three miles into Langley to get foot-long hot dogs at the Dog House Tavern. My mom bought a bag of healthy, hippie, potato chips at the Star Store and we all sat at the beach and ate our dinner. Most nights after work, my dad drank gin and tonic on the rocks and smoked his pot. My mom typically made some kind of dinner involving spinach, broccoli, potatoes, eggs, pork chops, and lots of butter; and occasionally liver and onions.

My mom had been happy taking care of us, but now I was ten and my brother was five and she wanted more for herself. Maybe she wanted independence. The Shell gas station in Clinton came up for rent and my parents and my Uncle Jim decided to lease it. My mom and Uncle Jim ran the station, while my dad continued selling real estate. The first thing my mom did was have our friend Shanti paint a big rainbow on the front window.

The Clinton Shell Station with the rainbow in the window, and the woman at the pump and in the garage caused quite a stir. My mom was a feminist. She loved running the station and the controversy it caused. For the most part her customers loved her and grew to respect her as a business woman.

During this time my parents' old friend Country Joe and his family came up to visit. My dad eventually sold Joe a house and small piece of property with a dock at Goss Lake. My mom and Joe had always had chemistry. My mom appreciated Joe's music and his politics. They sang and played guitar together.

One night when Joe was visiting the island, he and my mom drove up in my mom's big, dark-green Chevy panel van.

My dad, my brother, and I had been waiting for my mom. My mom went to work, my mom was in plays, but my mom never went out just for fun, so it was unusual for her not to be home. My mom and Joe had been out drinking, which was also unusual. I had never seen my mom drink. She was giggling and stumbling up to the house. She had a bottle of liquor in her hand. I was immediately enraged. Nothing about this was right.

"Mom."

"MOM."

"What are you doing?"

"Where were you?" I pleaded.

"Mom."

"MOM."

"Nothing, Cere," she said.

"Everything is fine."

"Joe and I were just hanging out."

"Mom."

"MOM." I pleaded more.

I took the bottle out of her hand. I smashed it down on the cement floor of the covered porch. Glass and liquor sprayed all over me and her.

I was crying.

I hated her.

I hated whatever was happening.

She was leaving me.

After that night we didn't see Joe for a while; and I never saw my mom drink again.

My mom began coming home later and later from the gas station. When she'd finally arrive home, my parents would fight in the kitchen while my brother and I pressed our ears to the door trying to listen and figure out what they were fighting about.

My mom was changing.

She was distracted.

She was busy.

She was unavailable.

My dad was mad at her all the time. I could see him tensing up each night as she came home later and later. He rarely had nice things to say about her.

He criticized her friends.

He criticized the gas station.

He criticized everything about her.

My mom fought back. She did not agree with his negative opinions about her or her friends. She did not agree with his chronic judgment and disdain for her or the people she cared about. He was relentless in his, I-am-better-than-you-attitude. She noticed he was starting to be more critical of me, too. He had a way of making her and me feel like we weren't good enough. He made us feel like we were wrong. He did this with his cutting words and harsh tone of voice.

When my mom made pancakes he would critique her, telling her the way she smashed them down was wrong, and his tone would be condescending and unforgiving. With me, when I would say "I know, I know" or "what?" he would ridicule me saying, "you think you know everything?" or "don't say 'what' to me, listen the first time." He was so convincing I found myself believing the things he said about her, me and the others in our family and community he criticized. It was mentally exhausting and left me doubting myself and feeling unloved by him. It never seemed like he liked me or my mom.

When my parents decided they needed some space from each other, I felt some relief initially. It was 1979 and they wanted to be progressive. They had a friend with a cabin and they each took one night a week in the cabin for themselves to think about their marriage and work on themselves. It was confusing for me, but I still trusted them.

We listened to Fleetwood Mac, the Eagles, Jackson Brown, Carol King, Joni Mitchell, Country Joe, Joan Baez, and Holly Near, loud on the stereo. My mom sang every word of every song. She seemed to be in her own world and continued to come home late from work. Then one night when my mom was supposed to be at the cabin, she forgot to call me. She always called me at nine to tell me goodnight. I lay in bed and waited for her to call as the nausea rolled over me.

I got up.
She didn't call.

I called the cabin number.
She didn't answer.
I felt sicker.

I hated her.
Where was she?
Five, ten, fifteen minutes went by.
She always called.

"Dad, Dad, DAD!"
"Why hasn't mom called?" I asked.

"I don't know," he said.

Finally the phone rang.
I ran to answer it.

"Mom."
"Where were you?"

"I was at a friend's property," she said.

"Whose property?"

"Just a friend," she said.

"Who?" I asked angrily.

"His name's Bill Tucker," she answered.
"He comes into the gas station."

"Why were you there?" I was confused.

"He had a bonfire and I just went to hang out," she said.

Silence.
Silence.
Silence.

"Ok, well, goodnight, honey."
"See you tomorrow."
"I love you," she said.

Silence was all I had.

I felt sick.
I wanted to scream.
I wanted to cry.
I was frozen.
I was eleven years old and in sixth grade with Mr. Posh. My brother was six. He was in first grade. That night changed everything. My mom came home the next night and I could tell at bedtime she was lying to me.
He was not a friend.
He was a boyfriend.

"I love you," she said, as she tucked me in bed.

"I hate you," I said.
It wasn't too long after that I got drunk on a whole bottle of champagne at a party. Of course the kids weren't supposed to be drinking, but we got ahold of a few bottles of champagne and instead of a little taste, like the other girls, I drank a whole bottle. My mom rubbed my back as I threw up in the toilet.
I felt completely out of control.
I felt disconnected from myself.
I felt terrified.
She was leaving me, again.

I begged and pleaded with my mom to stay. I begged and pleaded with her to keep the house. Every part of my being wanted to stay in that house on Saratoga Road and never leave. I was terrified that I wouldn't be able to survive the loss of my family, my house, and my childhood. It was all too much.

I loved every part of that house. I loved every part of my life in that house. Nothing would ever be the same. Nothing would ever be good like that again. My life was unraveling. I was unraveling. They were getting divorced.

I hated my mom for letting it all go.

I hated my mom for letting me go.

I hated everything.

I was in a fog.

I was watching my life unravel and I was looking for something to make me feel better. I was interested in boys and so were a lot of other sixth grade girls. We had crushes and some of us even had boyfriends. Most of us had been in school together since kindergarten. There were about ninety of us in sixth grade. It was our last year of elementary school. A week before school got out, our whole grade went on a four-day trip to Fort Casey, right by the Port Townsend ferry. It was an old army fort with barracks, hidden tunnels, canons, wide-open fields, and long stretches of beaches.

The girls slept in one barrack and the boys in the other. My romance with Glen began at some point before the trip. A spark ignited between us, but on the trip that spark became a flame. He started it. It was a mystery to me because even though we had been in class together throughout the years, we hadn't been particularly close friends.

That changed on the trip. We made eyes at one another, laughed, and flirted the entire time. We hung back away from the group and talked, held each other's sweaty hands, and even kissed on the long beach walk. I didn't know why he liked me and I didn't understand why I liked him, but there was never a doubt about our mutual attraction.

That summer I hung out with him and his older brother and sister at his old farmhouse and we met at the county fair.

At the fair we ran all over, flirting, teasing, talking, and holding hands. At night we went on the Zipper, sitting as close as we could. I bugged him and begged him to buy me a silver ring and he did. He also surprised me and bought a silver bracelet with two hearts connected by an arrow. He had our names engraved on the hearts.

I still have them both.

I broke up with him two weeks later, right before the first day of seventh grade. I wasn't exactly sure why, maybe the sadness about my parents' divorce, maybe the fear of caring about anybody too much or the feeling that he and I were too different and it wouldn't last. Whatever it was, I pulled completely away. I was heartbroken, but worst of all I felt I had broken his twelve-year-old heart, too.

I was working pretty hard at building a wall around myself. It didn't feel safe to care too much about anyone.

But I knew even then I loved him.

TWENTY-THREE

August 2005

The phone rings.
I'm still in bed.
I'm not quite awake.
It's Nate.

"Hi Mom, sorry I forgot your birthday."
"Happy birthday," he says.

"Thanks, Nate."

"I met a girl."
"Her name is Stacy."
"She's a lot like you."
"She's a massage therapist."

"That's so great," I said.
"But how is she like me?"

"She helps people."
"She is caring," he says.
"She is in acupuncture school."

"How did you meet her?" I ask.

"At a party in Bellingham."
"It was a luau."
"She lives in Arizona."
"She is friends with Andy's cousin."
"She's from Buffalo."
"She left this morning."

"I am going to go see her in two weeks," he explains. "Before I leave for Alaska."

"That's great."
"Sounds like you really like her," I offer.

"I do," he says.

"Thanks for calling, Nate."
"I love you."

"I love you too, Mom," he says and hangs up.

I breathe.

Nate hasn't sounded this happy since before Vida. I look over at the sepia photo I took of him when he was thirteen and on the Tiger football team. It sits by my bed in a frame that says: Sons, they fill our souls with pride… sons are charming… sons have courage. I sigh.

I say a prayer that this relationship, this woman, will lead Nate to sobriety. I wander out to the kitchen and put the red enamel kettle on the propane burner. I walk down the hall to Larry's office. I tell him about Nate's call and the news about the girlfriend, Stacy.

I hear the whistle of the teapot. I go back to the kitchen and make my strong black tea. Larry doesn't like coffee, so I changed to tea early on in our relationship, except on special occaisions. I miss my daily coffee and half-and-half. But coffee isn't the same when the other person isn't drinking it with you.

Vida is still asleep. I add organic 2% milk to my tea and take it out on the deck, in my white mug that says: *Peace, it does not mean to be where there is no trouble or hard work, it means to be amidst those things and still feel calm in your heart.* I hate mugs with words, but addiction has brought me this low. Like it or not, I am comforted by the words.

I absorb the warm August morning and the sound of

the birds singing. I look out at Larry's huge garden; it's almost a quarter of an acre. It is lush and every shade of green. It's surrounded by the dry yellow grasses of August. I marvel at the dozen fruit trees. The yellow plum trees are laden with fruit, the overabundance of the green pear trees and the apple trees, full and getting close to harvest. The nasturtiums and calendula border the garden, and the rows of veggies are long, green, and dense.

The basil is my favorite. Two long rows of basil growing thick like lettuce, with occasional purple blossoms indicating the need to harvest and have a pesto-making session. I am not a gardener, but I love having a garden.

Larry loves to garden.

I glance over at my office. I treasure the driftwood gate my friend Steven built and all the lavender, lilies, and Shasta daisies blooming inside the beds, enclosed by the rustic rock walls that June designed. The flowers and the path to my office are nurturing. The privacy, beauty, and peace it offers my clients and me is a gift.

I am also sad and run down. It's been three and half years of a living hell with Nate. I have not had a moment of true peace. Maybe this woman, Stacy, will change him. Does she know how bad he is? Maybe he's not as bad as I think. Maybe I am just an overreactive mother? Maybe it's because I am a therapist? Am I making things worse than they are? Maybe it's just in my head? Maybe I am grasping at straws?

I feel crazy.

I feel hopeful.

He seems to be in love.

That must be good.

My heart is beating faster.

I tell myself to just stay in the moment.

I tell myself not to worry.

I tell myself it's not in my hands.

I let go.
I put Nate in God's hands.
Nate falls out.
I put him in God's hands, again.
He falls out, again.
I pray for the next right thing to happen.

I breathe.

My high school reunion is in a couple of days. It makes me to puke. Even though I'm proud of myself and my life—I have a beautiful home on San Juan Island, I have a cabin on Demeter, I have a career I love, and a beautiful daughter—Nate is not doing so well. I am not ready to relive my adolescence all in one night. The truth is I've been avoiding it for twenty years.

I am not sure how interesting a reunion will be now that we are all on Facebook and already know what everyone is doing, what each other looks like, and who has children, etc. But Glen has called and he wants me to go.

I need a cigarette already.

I'm bringing Vida because Oliver is coming to Whidbey this weekend, too. My mom has rented a cabin at Maxwelton Beach for him and his family.

I don't want Larry to come. I feel awkward about our twenty-five year age difference and I don't think I can relax and be myself with him there. I don't want to feel this way. I want to feel proud of my husband. I want to dance the night away with the man I love.

That's not how it is.

Instead, I feel like I am seventeen again and I'm excited to spend time with Glen, as if none of the hurt and disappointment has ever come between us. As if I am not furious at the kind of father he has been. We haven't spent much more than ten minutes together since Nate was two. We slept together a couple of times when he visited us at Evergreen. We've talked briefly at Thanksgiving and Christmas when I dropped Nate off at his house or at the ferry terminal waiting room, on the rare occasion he had Nate for the weekend. We have, of course, talked about money over the years, usually about me wanting more from him. We've talked on the phone more recently about Nate and his addiction. But this is different. All those old feelings rise to the surface.

It's not a good thing.

I meet Glen at his house. Nate's there and so is Glen's son Garrett, who's ten. The cabin he is living in is on Bells Beach, one of our favorite beaches we escaped to when we were sixteen. The tide is way out. The beach is more beautiful than I remember. My old bus stop in front of Helen's Store is just up the hill. I'm flooded with memories of my childhood and our relationship. I don't say too much. Glen takes Vida on a walk down to the beach where the tide is way out, and he helps her find a sand dollar.

Later I meet up with my old friends Tia and Suzanne at Maxwelton Beach and I drive us all to the reunion, stopping on the way to buy a pack of Marlboro Lights.

It's as if we never left those summer nights, getting ready for the Bayview dances. We are giggly and nervous and full of ourselves, only now we are all thirty-eight years old and I am the frumpy one. Tia lives in LA with her daughter, Ava, and is way more hip than me or Suzanne. Suzanne is living in Magnolia and working for Microsoft. She has two children and is as beautiful as ever, with her long, red, loopy curls.

There are some surprises at the reunion, like my friend Annie from eighth grade. I love seeing and connecting with a few people that I had once been close to. But in true teenage fashion, I am preoccupied by Glen. I can't help myself. Even sober I am unable to manage my feelings for him, despite his temporary, tacky, alcoholic girlfriend sitting next to him.

Glen and his not-so-savory girlfriend drink too much. I

don't drink at all. I smoke. I drive them home to Bells Beach. It's weird. But I don't really care. When we arrive, she goes into the house. Glen and I stay outside and talk for a minute. He pulls me toward him.

He kisses me.

My heart beats fast. It's wrong. I pull away and tell him no. I turn him towards his front door and leave. I drive up Bells Beach Road and down Saratoga into Langley. I try to put myself back together before I climb into bed at my mom's and fall asleep next to Vida.

I opt to skip the family part of the reunion the next day. We hang out with my brother for most of Sunday. We stop by one more time at Glen's to say goodbye to him and to Nate. They are leaving for Alaska any day. Vida and I drive to Anacortes and catch the last boat home.

I am a wreck. And there is nothing I can do about it. I'm just going to be a wreck for a while. I can't deal with him. I'm married to Larry.

Glen is dangerous. I'm dangerous. He still drinks. It's all just a really bad idea. I do my best to start tucking it all away. I want these feelings to disappear. I can't afford to unravel, not now, not like this. I call June and she meets me in town. We sit in her little truck. I unravel, for a moment.

I smoke one more cigarette.

I breathe, sort of.

TWENTY-FOUR

1979

Seventh grade began and my mom moved my brother and me into a small rental near Bells Beach. It was a very angry, angry time for me. I was angry for good reason; besides losing my home and family, I had lost trust in my mother.

She was consumed with her divorce, her romance, and her new job running the South Whidbey Children's Center. I had no empathy for her whatsoever. It didn't help that my dad was so negative towards her, and that he shared his feelings and his side of the story with me, whenever he had the chance.

My dad felt very wounded by the divorce. However, he had been having an affair on and off with Libby from the time I was two and he was always so hard on my mom. His double standards were exhausting.

My brother and I were going back and forth between my parents and their two cramped cabin rentals.

One horrible day, my friend Ursula found her mom bleeding to death from slitting her wrists in the tiny bathroom of their red Baby Island cabin. The ambulance, my mom, and I came and Jeanne was taken to the hospital. Ursula was going to live with us.

Jeanne had a severe drinking problem, an addiction, which made life for Ursula painful and difficult. She had tried to stay sober, but it never worked for very long. After this suicide attempt, Jeanne had to stay sober or she would temporarily lose Ursula to the state. Her alcoholism was too destructive. While she was committed to Northern State, we drove Ursula to visit.

Visiting that old, cement mental hospital in Sedro-Wooley was surreal. Even in 1980 it was broken down. The building was cold, sterile, and falling apart. Patients shuffled down the halls. Some were schizophrenic, others depressed, bipolar or struggling with addiction. I felt strong, unafraid, and curious. I could feel the suffering emanating from the pasty white walls, and the severity of each individual's situation, which brought them to these halls. I felt the weight of it, but not nearly the weight that Ursula felt, having her own mother one of the patients.

It was there that I first learned about addiction. On one of our visits, my mom, Ursula, Jeanne, and I watched a movie that featured a woman making toast. If the toast was burnt she took a drink to feel better, and if the toast was perfect she took a drink to celebrate. For a person who struggled with addiction, every occasion was an occasion to drink. It didn't matter what was happening in their life. Their drinking was not caused by outside events.

It was a disease.

It was no one's fault.

TWENTY-FIVE

Winter 2006

Nate is bringing Stacy home to meet me after Christmas. It's been four months since they met at the luau in Bellingham. I am anxious to meet this woman.

This woman who is like me. This woman who has my son talking about houses and big living-room couches. This woman whom he makes an effort to see. This woman, whom a friend tells me, the moment Nate laid eyes on her he turned and said, I'm going to marry that girl. They hadn't even spoken.

This is the woman he is delivering to me in a matter of hours. They will be coming in on the late ferry, and in the morning Stacy and I will have a few hours to visit, before they leave on the one o'clock ferry.

They arrive late. I've already been dozing on the couch. They come in and I welcome her with a warm hug. She has dyed reddish hair, big blue eyes, a long neck, and an enthusiastic toothy smile. She is tall, much taller than I am, and almost as tall as Nate. She is pretty much a spitting image of Julia Roberts. I can feel that she is kind and loving from the moment she enters the house. We make a plan to go on a hike, just the two of us. Nate insists that I spend time alone with her. Maybe he just doesn't want to go on a hike.

I wake up around eight and make my cup of tea with milk and a half teaspoon of brown sugar. I sit on the couch looking out at the valley, waiting for Stacy to wake.

When she wakes she has a cup of tea with me. She still wants to go on the hike. We get dressed and head out Cattlepoint Road to Mount Finlayson in my white Volvo wagon with the seat warmers. It's winter, but it's not raining.

We park, put on our hand-knit hats, zip up our coats, and start down the path through the woods. This is my favorite path to take with Vida. There is something about starting down that long hill and slowly making our way through the forest, then up the steep gnome hill, until we pop out at the top and look down at the ocean waves curving all the way down South Beach.

Lately, I have been in a hiking mood. I find out later it's one of Stacy's favorite pastimes. She has sweet memories from childhood, hiking with her dad. It was the perfect choice for us that morning.

I'm used to listening, so by the time we are hiking she has shared with me a lot about herself. Her work as a massage therapist, her schooling to become an acupuncturist, her recent divorce, her parents' divorce, and her struggles as a teenage girl on her own in Buffalo. She finished massage school by the time she was seventeen. She's twenty-three now, three years older than Nate.

As we walk and talk it is easy, like talking with an old friend. I am impressed with her apparent strength and insight into her own life. She is very much on her own in the world. She is striving to live a healthy life. Her marriage had not been healthy and she is wanting something better for herself.

I'm head over heels. I adore her. I'm completely confused as to why this exceptional young woman would have any interest in my son. He has a car, but no license. He has a job, but no home. He has problems with alcohol, cocaine, and other drugs. What could Stacy possibly see in him?

"Why do you like Nate?" I ask her.

"He's emotionally available," she says.

"Really?" I have a hard time believing her.

"Yes," she says.
"He can talk about the relationship."
"He can talk about his feelings."

"Okay," I say.

As a therapist and mother of a son, that's one of the more remarkable things she could have said. Emotionally available, isn't that the whole point? I believe he has revealed this part of himself to her. I also believe they have a long, hard road ahead.

We finish the hike and drive back to the house. Nate is waiting for us. He is ready to go. I thank him for bringing her to me. I tell him she is amazing. I give them both big hugs and say goodbye as they rush for the ferry. Vida and I watch from the porch as they drive off.

I'm in love.

I hope she stays.

TWENTY-SIX

2006

It's May 2006 and Stacy has rented a U-Haul and a storage unit in Anacortes. She is moving to Washington. Nate has asked if they can live with us on Lampard. I am hesitant. Stacy brings her black pitbull, Mara. I am not too thrilled about any of it, except for Stacy.

I want to say yes.

I want to be supportive of their relationship.
I want to believe that things will be normal now.
I want to believe Nate will stop using now.
I want to believe that these are things Stacy will bring.
I underestimate the problem.
I overestimate Stacy's influence.

I let them live with us.

Nate and I are having a lot of conflict about his car. He hasn't been making his payments. Since I am on the title, this affects me. I want to get off the title of his Xterra. Nate has bad credit, so he can't get a new car on his own. Stacy has good credit. After moving into the bright-blue room they take the ferry to Burlington, trade/in the Xterra and come back with a brand new, black 2006 Dodge Caliber with tinted windows.

They love it.
I hate it.

When they pick up Vida from kindergarten, with Mara's head sticking out the tinted window, Stacy in her spiky high heels and Nate in his sagging jeans, my friends say the other kindergarteners think they are rock stars. I think they look like drug dealers.

I am not happy.

Nate leaves for Alaska and Stacy stays with us. Life is calmer without him here. Stacy has a couch, a bed, and a whole house full of furniture in her storage unit. She finds a house in Anacortes and waits for Nate to send his first paycheck home. She rents the house on Sterling Street, just a mile up the hill as you drive off the ferry in Anacortes. She packs up the bright blue room on the first of July and moves into the new house.

I breathe.

I stay in touch with Stacy. She finds a job at a hotel spa doing massage. She visits us every couple of weeks. We develop a sweet rapport. I'm afraid to get too attached. Nate comes home from fishing in August. They tell me over the phone they are engaged.

By September they are pregnant. Stacy is ecstatic, Nate too. I am cautiously optimistic. I love babies, but I don't think they are ready for one. I am afraid that with Nate's addiction, there is no way this baby's needs will be met.

My body is tense.

My heart hurts.

I hold my breath.

I feel separate from Nate. I want to feel separate from Stacy, but she is carrying my grandbaby. She also seems to have very little family support, emotional or financial.

I slowly realize I do need to pay attention. These are new roles for Stacy and me. I begin to think of Stacy as part of the family. I make sure to include her in Vida's birthday, Thanksgiving, and Christmas. I want her to feel welcome and safe in our family. I do not want her to feel alone. I do not want her to feel alone with this baby or alone with Nate's addiction.

Nate goes fishing.

Nate comes home again.

I pull him aside.

"You can't keep using."

"This won't work."

"You need to either stop fishing or get on a clean boat," I tell him.

Out of desperation, I joke, "You are going to have to become a born-again Christian fisherman."

"That's the only way I see this working."

"Mom, I'm not using," he lies.
"Mom, it's fine."

"I can see it's not fine," I say.
"You have no money."
"Stacy needs support."
"You are going to be a father."
"You are still hanging out with people who use."
"You can't keep living like this."
"You either need to quit fishing, get sober, or become a Christian," I beg him.

"Okay Mom, whatever."
"That's not going to happen."
"I am not going to become a Christian."
"I'll be a good dad," he says.

"I hope so, Nate."
"I really hope so."

I'm angry. I can see that he is not taking his new role as a dad seriously. He is proud, but he is not connected to the reality of the situation. He is distracted by his addiction. He drives around without a license in their black Dodge Caliber with tinted windows and their pitbull in the back. He drives too fast. He drives with the base too high and volume too loud. He goes to the store and takes hours to return. He smokes. He chews tobacco. He drinks energy drinks. He's either hyped up and agitated or he's sleeping.

On the way to drop Nate off at the airport for his next trip to Alaska, Stacy hits a patch of black ice on I-5 near Stanwood. The car does a three-sixty and spins off the road. They miss hitting another car and a tree. They could have died. Stacy could have miscarried. They are lucky. Nate is always lucky. This is not a good thing.

This is how things go when you are using. It's always something. I have learned not to put energy into these accidents or events. In my mind, they are all a result of addiction. It's the ongoing chaos and the inability for anyone close to the addiction to think or act in a clear, reliable way. I see that big red stamp of addiction all over it.

I feel sad.

I feel angry.

I feel powerless.

I feel detached.

I say the Serenity Prayer.

I am relieved when Nate goes fishing.

I know life will be calmer for at least sixty days.

It's January. Larry, Vida, and I spend New Year's on Demeter. Winter in the cabin is cozy and warm. Our bed and Vida's are arranged in the living room and I read piles of books to Vida.

We walk down the trail to visit Alison, Sonja, and Iris. Alison and I drink tea while the girls rummage through boxes of dress-up clothes and perform elaborate plays for us. When the bickering gets too much, Vida and I walk home in the dark, with just the moon to light our path. I end up carrying her through the darkest parts of the woods until we see the faint light of our cabin. Larry is already in bed.

We brush our teeth at the faucet outside, take the flashlight to the outhouse and run in the cabin and put on our jammies. I tuck her into her little bed with her favorite blankies and her doll Josephina. I sing to her and stay until we both fall asleep.

When I return from Demeter, I call Stacy.

"How are you feeling?"

"I am not feeling good."
"I can't eat."
"I can't drink."
"I throw up all day," she reports.

"What are you doing?" I ask.
"Have you called your midwives?"

"I haven't."
"I am lying on the couch."
"I can't really move."

"Is there anyone in Anacortes that can help you?" I ask.

"Maybe Wendy," she offers.

"Can you call her?"
"Or should I?"
"I think you need to go to the hospital," I say.

"Can you?" she asks.

"Yes, give me her number."
I look up some of Stacy's symptoms on the internet. She appears to have a condition that some women get when they are pregnant, which goes beyond the normal morning sickness. It's called hyperemesis gravidarum. It causes dehydration and low iron, which makes it almost impossible to keep food or liquids down. It's a difficult cycle to break.
Shit.
I can't stay detached.
I have to fully attach.
I have to care more than I want to.

I have to parent Stacy.

I have to help.

I don't want to.

I don't want to be in this situation. I have worked so hard to detach from Nate, his choices, and his life of addiction. I have to go back in because it's not just Stacy and Nate. There is a baby and that baby has needs.

I don't want the chaos of addiction in my life.

I don't want that sick feeling in my gut.

But more than what I don't want, what I do want is this baby to have everything it needs. I refuse to leave Stacy alone.

I walk on the ferry. She picks me up at the ferry landing. We go to her midwife appointments at the Bellingham Birth Center. We drive all over Anacortes looking at garage sales for the things she wants and needs for the baby's room.

We have fun.

We shop at the fancy fabric store and choose colors, patterns, and a design for the quilt I am going to sew for the baby. I have never made a real quilt with little squares sewn perfectly straight. I treat her like she is my daughter, only without any history or struggle, so it's easier for both of us.

She works. She tries to eat. She drinks her liquids in very small doses. She makes their little house a home and makes the second bedroom into a sweet nursery. Everything she chooses is thoughtful, sweet, and simple. She turns the third room into into a mother-in-law space for me. She always makes me feel welcome. I am still careful not to intrude or do too much.

I love her.

I want her to be in charge.

This is her family, not mine.

I decide I need to take better care of myself if I am going to be a grandma at thirty-nine. I start covering my grey. I add miles to my running during the winter.

I have run more miles at one time then I ever thought

possible. I am spending more time on myself than I have in a long time, if ever. I savor the early morning runs before Vida wakes.

For me the running is more than simply exercise and stress release. It becomes about challenging my own mind and body to do something that I am not entirely sure is possible. I decide to run a marathon with my friend Kerry. I decided to do it for Stacy, too. I see the marathon as a metaphor for giving birth.

I run. It hurts. It feels euphoric, too. Kerry and I talk. We talk about our children. I talk about Nate, about his addiction and my worries for Stacy and the baby. I am still compartmentalizing, being careful about what I share and don't share about myself. I mostly listen.

Kerry talks about herself, her childhood being raised Mormon, and her marriage. I encourage her to tell the truth about how she feels, about what she needs and wants in her marriage, in her life.

I share some of my worries about my own marriage. We talk about sex. We talk about the importance of marriage and commitment, for our girls, for our families, and even for ourselves.

The running is hard.

The thinking is harder.

The feeling is the hardest.

I am tired of being married or at least tired of trying to make everyone happy. I have been with Larry for fourteen years and a mom for twenty-two.

I'm exhausted.

I have not yet allowed myself time to even consider being tired. I have kept that feeling, those resentments, all of those inconvenient feelings tucked away. I have hidden them, even from myself.

Running with Kerry exposes some of those loose threads. I'm not ready to admit to her or anyone else, but on those long runs I cannot defend against them. I tell myself I'm committed to staying in my marriage, but I might not be telling the truth.

The start of the race is at Deception Pass.

I'm nervous.

Actually, I'm terrified.

I meet Kerry at the start. I don't throw up, but I feel like it. Our plan is to go slow and steady. I run down the island I was raised on, yet running on parts of it I had never seen. Kerry stays with me. She runs whatever pace I run. She walks when I need to walk. She rests when I need to rest. Finally we make it, with remarkably little strain, to mile twenty-three.

My calves cramp. We have three miles left. I feel like I am being stabbed with knives in my calves. I think of Stacy preparing to give birth in June. I remember the pain of labor. I can do this. Kerry is patient. She encourages me. She runs in front of me, coaxing me along. I want to stop so badly. She tells me I can do it. I believe her. I run backwards, that feels better.

I rest.

I walk.

I run backwards.

I want to cry.

I think of Stacy.

I think of Nate.

I think of Ryan.

I think of Tony.

I think of my clients and the pain they have experienced in their lives. This pain is nothing in comparison. This is pain I've chosen. It's not really pain. It's a metaphor for pain.

I rest.

I walk.

I run backwards.

I want to cry.

I think of Stacy.

I run.

I breathe.

I can finally see the finish line. Kerry and I run down the gently sloping hill and through the finish line with no hesitation. I have a surge of new energy, a big smile of relief. Stacy is there to greet me.

Stacy drives me back to my car at Deception Pass. I speed down Marine Drive towards the ferry. I ease my car down lane four with that familiar relief that I'll be on the next ferry. My body relaxes for the first time all day or maybe longer.

I feel different.

I feel strong.
I feel sore.
I feel tired.

I want to go home.
I want to snuggle up with my girl.

I breathe.

TWENTY-SEVEN

1982

I never wanted to be home.

Home didn't feel like home anymore.

Home felt like a place I was waiting to leave.

I moved between my parents' two homes every other week until I couldn't take it anymore. My mom's was just plain lonely. She left for work at six in the morning and didn't get home from the Children's Center until six or seven at night. Around eleven o'clock every night, she drove a few blocks to the Clinton Laundromat to clean and lock up. She also waitressed at La Casita a night or two a week. She was always working, at meetings or on the phone. At least the boyfriend was gone.

She was doing her best to make enough money to support my brother and me. My dad wasn't helping financially. All the reasons didn't matter to me. What mattered was that my mom wasn't home.

I hated it.

I hated her.

I missed my old mom.

I missed my mom before the divorce.

I missed the mom who was there.

The mom I could count on.

I left my mom's and moved into my dad's full time. He was more lenient, and more available, and I had my own room, even though it didn't have a door and the floor was plywood and the sheetrock was unfinished. My mom didn't want me to move. She protested and tried to stop me, but she couldn't convince me otherwise.

She couldn't stop me, so she followed me. She moved into the studio apartment that my dad had built on the bottom floor. My mom wasn't willing to let me go, as much as I tried to push her away.

I looked for home everywhere and with everyone. I thought I might find it in a boy or in bottle. Sometimes a cigarette in the school parking lot felt like home. Other times smoking pot and skipping French class felt like home.

At night, I hitchhiked home from parties at the end of long dirt roads and in abandoned fields. The parties were in old, run-down trailers in the woods. I drank too much. I ended up in back rooms and back seats with senior boys doing things I had only heard referenced in movies or in books. Those things always ended with me naked.

Some of the guys were already out of high school. They drank, a lot. They lived in dirty travel trailers in their parents' backyards. I never really understood how I ended up in those trailers, with those men; I just know I did. There was no embarrassment at school after those nights, just a private shame that I had to tuck into places inside myself, where I hoped they could never escape.

I was looking for a way to feel different and better. When alcohol and pot grew too familiar, I tried speed: black beauties and diet pills. I liked the feeling of speed. I liked the way I felt with no appetite. I liked the way it felt to be hovering above ground, just a little bit. I liked the way it felt to throw up if I ate too much.

I liked feeling in control.

I became familiar with feeling a bit light-headed from too much Diet Pepsi and Red Vines and not enough real food. I fainted in the shower once. When I came to, I dried myself off and went to school. I never mentioned it.

More than anything, I savored the feeling of my body growing thinner. My stomach became flatter than ever before. As summer approached I obsessed about how I looked in my black crocheted bikini. I laid on the dock at Deer Lake drinking beer, smoking Marlboro Lights, feeling thin and sexy.

I felt different at work, too. I was a sales clerk on the clothing side of the Star Store and a barista and waitress at Angelina's Bakery.

I felt grown up.

I felt in control.

I felt competent.

At work I had everything I needed, and I had money to take care of myself.

I relished the freedom of having my own money. I wanted to be in charge of myself. Tia and I decided we should live on our own. We devised a plan and told our parents.

It was February, we were fifteen and sophomores in high school. We planned to live in the cabin behind Tia's mom's house on First Street. We would pay her a small amount of rent and do everything ourselves. My parents tried to say no. I told them I was going to do it whether they liked it or not.

They gave in.

I borrowed my dad's friend Charlie's red 1960's Ford pickup truck. I loaded up my bedroom furniture and clothes and we drove over to Tia's mom's house. We lived there for two months. I woke up early, walked down the hill to the bakery and opened it on Sunday mornings. Being the first one there I'd make myself a cappuccino, watch the teaspoon of brown sugar melt and sink through the thick foam, then sip it while I baked. I shaped and boiled the bagels and made quiche from scratch. When I worked dinners at the bakery, my boss, who always seemed to stand a little too close, taught me the skills of a good waitress and let me taste the wine after closing.

It only lasted two months. Tia's dad made her move back with him in Everett. Her mom had Multiple Sclerosis and was getting sicker and Tia couldn't stay on Whidbey. I was sad to see Tia go. Life was hard and moving fast for both of us.

I was hell-bent on not moving home, so I found another little cottage to rent. It was on the same back alley as Tia's mom's. I kept working, going to school, and somewhat managing my independent teenage life. I got a puppy.

My mom insisted we have dinner once a week. We ate at La Casita. It was our favorite Mexican restaurant and was in the old drive-in, Snack Shack, across from Langley High School. We ate chips and cheese with jalapeños and diced tomatoes, while I worked at keeping the wall I had built between us from falling down.

One late spring night after work, I was walking through Langley and heading to my little house on the alley between First and Second Street, and saw some guys hanging out by their trucks. Glen was there and our eyes met. We both smiled in recognition, as if we had been looking for one another. His bright blue eyes shined and his skin was tan.

I hadn't seen him since the end of seventh grade. I didn't know where he had been. It had been almost three years since his dad died on his thirteenth birthday. He had crashed his motorcycle on Baby Island Road as he was on his way home. After that, his mom moved him to Las Vegas to live with his sister, but now they were back. I felt guilty that I had never even talked to him about his dad dying.

There was no hesitation, our bodies gravitated toward one another. We couldn't stop talking or touching. Before I knew it we were walking up the alley, the moonlight shining down on us. At my little cottage we left the lights off and climbed into bed. There was no awkwardness, no doubts, no question of what we would do. We just knew. It was that way between us.

But in the rest of our world it was complicated. One of us was always holding back or in another relationship. There were external barriers and this time was no different.

I didn't want to love him, but I did.

TWENTY-EIGHT

Summer 2007

We gather over fifty friends and family at the house for a barbecue and baby shower to celebrate Nate, Stacy, and their baby on the way. It is a hot, sunny day with kids running around in the yard, babies in arms, pregnant bellies, hula hooping, and belly measuring. Larry grills fresh salmon and my spicy, apricot, glazed chicken. I make a big caesar salad and we have lemonade.

The house is full of love.

I am grateful, yet heavy hearted knowing Nate is not clean and neither are most of his friends. I do my best to lift them up. I focus on the good, even though I know it isn't all that good. In the back of my mind, I think if I just keep loving him, loving Stacy, and loving this baby on the way, that maybe the love and boundaries will bring healing and wholeness to our family.

I smile.

I pretend.

I give.

I breathe.

The next day we all go to Eagle Cove. It is a long and beautiful day with low tide and rising fog. There is bocce ball, tide-pooling, wading, skim-boarding, chatting about the baby-to-be and hiking the long trail up to the car, which may have induced Stacy's labor.

Now it's five in the afternoon and we've been making yellow and blue lupine flower wreaths on the deck. Nate, Stacy,

Vida, and I are walking around the house with the flower wreaths on our heads. Everyone is happy, but tired. Stacy thinks she may really be in labor.

The next ferry leaves at six. We need to catch that ferry and drive Stacy to the Bellingham Birth Center. My mom is here to be an extra support for Vida so I can be at the birth. Stacy's stepmom Eileen, who is a midwife, has flown out from Buffalo to be at the birth.

Nate has already flown home from fishing after Stacy had false labor a few weeks ago, when she was in Buffalo.

We drive right on the ferry. Stacy has to pause during contractions, but she can still talk in between them. This is the weekend every year that the barber shop quartet comes out to the island and they are leaving on the same ferry. They see us all sitting there in a booth. We tell them Stacy is in labor. They sing a special song to her, Nate, and the baby. By the end of the song, we all have tears streaming down our cheeks.

We arrive forty-five minutes later at the birth center.

Stacy breathes.

I wait.

Nate sleeps.

Stacy breathes.

Stacy walks.

The midwives stay with her.

The night is long.

Stacy is quiet.

In the early morning the midwives come to get Eileen and me from the waiting room. We go back into the birthing room. Nate is barely awake. He must be on painkillers to be practically sleeping through the birth of his first child. He just lays there, eyes half closed. His nose is reddish. His skin is blotchy. He doesn't seem connected to anything that is going on. It's a birth, there is a lot to connect to and there is a barrier between him and all of us. He seems unaware but half-heartedly trying. I motion for him to help Stacy. He sits behind her as she squats on the birthing stool. The baby's head is crowning.

Stacy pushes.

Stacy breathes.

Stacy screams.

Finally, a sweet, small miracle of a baby slips out of Stacy and into the midwives hands. The relief in the room is palpable. A healthy, baby boy. He's perfect. Nate says Stacy sounded like a pterodactyl. We laugh, even the midwives and even Stacy.

I love Stacy and Carter.

I give them my whole heart.

Nate is on his own.

Within a month, Nate leaves for Alaska and Stacy is home alone in Anacortes with a newborn baby and not enough money. He rarely leaves Stacy with money when he goes fishing. I visit Stacy. There are mostly condiments in the fridge and barely any food in the cupboards. There is no money, either.

I buy groceries, fill the fridge.

We talk about what it was like to grow up at times with only condiments in her fridge. I tell her that it's not okay. It was not okay then and it's not okay now. She has to have food in her fridge, for herself and her baby. I talk about the importance of nurturing herself so she can nurture this baby. I talk about how serious Nate's addiction is. I talk about how it isn't changing. I am worried for her. I am worried for Carter. I think she should leave.

She listens.

She thinks.

She stays, anyway.

When Stacy was first pregnant, we went to Bellingham to look at mattresses. After we picked out the mattress, Nate left Stacy and me at TJ Maxx to buy bedding. He had to run an errand. Hours later, Stacy and I were still sitting in front of TJ Maxx, with no sign of Nate. Stacy was practically in tears and I was furious. I knew the reason he was late had something to do with drugs. It's all, always, about addiction.

I told Stacy, if I were you I would run, not walk, as far away from Nate as you can. I tell her about Glen and how I had to shut him out to survive. I tell her I could not deal with the chaos, absence and lies that go hand in hand with addiction. I tell her I will love her and support her no matter what she does. I will do anything to support her in being a good mom. I will not support Nate and his addiction.

Nate finally showed up. Stacy was angry. I was angry. Nate was hyped up and full of excuses. The music was blaring and the bass was pounding Lil' Wayne on the car stereo. I had walked on the ferry as usual, so I had no car. I was trapped. We drove for half an hour up a long, steep dirt road to some random guy's house in the woods. I was still in the backseat. My stomach churning and anger building.

At the house there were shady deals and too many pitbulls. I hated that I was there. I hated that I was a part of any of it. I hated it even worse that Stacy was there and Stacy was a part of it. I hated that this was what Nate, my son, was about. He backed down the dirt driveway and hit a tree. Stacy felt even sicker. We were both trapped in this fucked up drug world with Nate.

I couldn't wait to go home.

Stacy stays.

Nate finally sends money home and Stacy's fridge stays full of good food to nurture her nursing body. Nate and she talk every day while he's on the boat. They get along better when he's fishing.

I help around the house. I wash dishes, fold laundry, hold Carter, change diapers, and run errands. I will basically do anything Stacy wants or needs. I am happy to help. Stacy takes good care of Carter and the house.

Stacy comes to visit us, too.

Vida is a good auntie. She will soon be in first grade. She loves Carter, but misses me. Having me gone once a week isn't her favorite thing. Me being in love with another baby isn't her favorite thing, either. That first day when Vida met Carter, Nate looks over at her and says, "Vida, now you know how I felt when you came. I was jealous. It was hard to share Mom."

I do everything I can to assure Vida and keep showing her that she is my first priority. I explain to Vida how important it is that Stacy is not alone. I explain to her that I don't know how long Stacy will live so close. I need to help Stacy now because she is here now and needs my help now. Vida tries hard to understand. She tries hard not to miss me. But it's impossible.

Sometimes when I visit Stacy and Carter, Larry takes Vida on the boat to Demeter. She has fun when she gets there, but it makes her anxious to go on the boat without me. If it's stormy or the tides are strong, the boat can get rocky and scary for her. She doesn't eat very much when I am gone. She's terrified I won't come back. I listen to her feelings. I stay close to her when I am home. I bring her with me when I can.

Sometimes on my weekly ferry ride, friends and acquaintances question me about why I go to see my grandson every week. I tell them, I go because I can. I tell them, you never know when you won't be able to see the people you love. I tell them, I am doing what feels right, even if it doesn't make sense.

It's a peaceful and healing time for me. Nate can't accept my love right now, nor is he easy to love, but Stacy and Carter can. Stacy brings out the best in me, is easy to love and I rediscover parts of myself that have been tucked away in my marriage.

I feel real.

I feel alive.

I feel blessed, too.

Stacy is a gentle and patient mother. She is thoughtful

and intentional in the way she takes care of Carter. It's a privilege to be a witness to her mothering. She has a loving heart. Everything I give her she uses, she multiplies, she makes better. I learn from her. I love her like a daughter.

But she and Nate need help that I can't give them. I encourage them to go to church. Glen's sister is married to a pastor. They are founders of a church in Anacortes. One Sunday I take Nate, Stacy, and Carter to the church. The sermon is on the Prodigal Son. The son makes mistakes and returns to the father. Instead of reprimanding him the father welcomes him back with open arms and unconditional love.

I pray.

I pray for God to work in Nate's life.

I pray for the next right thing to happen.

I pray.

We all try to change Nate.

Nate continues to use.

He continues to fish.

He continues to lay on the couch half asleep.

He continues to go to the "store" and not return for hours and hours.

He continues to spend all the money.

He continues to be angry.

I make it clear to Stacy and Nate that no matter what happens between them, I am keeping Stacy. I tell Nate that Stacy will be at our house every Christmas whether he is with her or not. I tell him not to fuck it up.

I hope he gets it together.

I hope she stays, for our sake.

For her sake, I hope she leaves.

For Christmas, Nate is fishing. Nothing is better. He isn't sober. He isn't changing. He isn't close to being the dad that

Carter needs. I don't let that get in my way of loving Stacy and Carter. We grow closer. I spend a little more time with them when Stacy starts working a couple of days a week.

I watch Carter.

Stacy and Carter stay at our house for a few days. Under the tree is a small box from her. I open it and inside is a little piece of paper folded up. I unfold it and on the paper it says, another grand-baby.

"What?"

"You're pregnant?"

"Carter's only six months old," I say.

"Yep." She gives me a half smile.

"Are you sure?"

"Are you sure you want to stay pregnant?"

"Yep."

"It'll be okay," she says.

I don't know how, but I say, "Okay."

I take a deep breath.

"Well, congratulations!"

"Two babies," I do the math, "fourteen months apart."

"Almost Irish twins."

"It's gonna be crazy."

"It's gonna be hard. "

"I know," she concedes.

We both breathe.

TWENTY-NINE

August 1984

I asked my dad if I could move back home on my sixteenth birthday. He said he would let me move home, but I had to pay a hundred dollars a month in rent and get rid of my puppy.

That fall I felt a sense of relief being home.

I focused on school until spring of that year, when I started getting restless and began hanging out with friends again. We drove around looking for boys day and night. We skipped school. We smoked. We drank. We stayed out all night and giggled uncontrollably.

On one of those late nights, we ran into Glen. All those old feelings were swarming between us. He was living with his brother in Langley, just a couple of miles away from my dad's, and we rekindled our relationship.

I was waitressing nights in Freeland at the Purple Parrot, a Mexican restaurant. When I got off work, I drove to whatever party he was at or to his house. He'd put on the Elton John album; "Tiny Dancer," "Norma Jean," and "Your Song," played as we stretched out on his double bed talking and eventually having sex. We'd fall asleep, our bodies sweaty and intertwined with each other and the sheets. Around two or three in the morning, I'd reluctantly drive home and climb into my own bed. It was dreamy and I was needy. I wanted so badly for things to be good and easy between us.

But they were never easy. Glen's drinking was the only thing that caused conflict between us, and that summer he seemed to be drinking more. He was hanging out with an older crowd. I thought he was doing coke. There was a girl she kept mentioning, too. It was driving me crazy. I didn't trust him. It caused a lot of fighting between us. He was pushing me away, even though I knew he loved me. I had done the same thing to him.

My parents were both out of town when I threw Glen a seventeenth birthday party. More people showed up than I expected. One of the big windows was broken when a champagne cork hit it at full speed. I didn't notice until morning, when I saw the shattered window.

When everyone left or was asleep, Glen and I were in my dad's room and ended up in a big fight. Glen punched a hole in the wall, he was so mad at me and drunk. I had never been scared of him before. I couldn't be with someone who I couldn't trust, who drank too much and who punched holes in walls.

We broke up.

One night at the end of August I stopped by Glen's on the way home from work. We hadn't seen each other in a few weeks and although it felt right to be apart, I missed him. I knew he missed me, too.

It was late. He welcomed me into his bed. He put on the Elton John record and we found that familiar place between us. Our relationship had always been rough, with mixed messages and hurt feelings. But when we were at our best, I didn't have to hold myself together or keep everything inside.

I soaked him in.

I savored us.

I breathed.

I imagined staying in that moment forever. I fell asleep with his arms wrapped around me and "Tiny Dancer" softly humming in the background.

I woke up around four in the morning and drove myself home. I climbed the stairs to my bedroom and fell back asleep. I woke late in the morning in a panic. I hadn't told Glen that I went off my birth control pills two weeks ago. Was I pregnant? I'd had pregnancy scares before, but this felt different. In my gut I knew, even though I couldn't really know.

I drove to Glen's. I was clear that our relationship couldn't work, between his drinking, my lack of trust, and our fighting. The love between us didn't matter. I couldn't see how I could function in my own life and deal with his.

I told him. He was hurt. He was angry. He told me how much he loved me. He wanted me to change my mind. He promised me he'd drink less and he'd be the kind of boyfriend I wanted, needed, deserved. He said everything I had ever wanted him to say. But my wall was already up. I didn't believe in him or us.

I couldn't stay.
I was abandoning him.
I was saving myself.

Both our hearts were breaking.
The pain was deep.
It was everywhere.

I cried.
I couldn't stop.
I hated every second.

It's not what I wanted.
It was what I had to do.
I couldn't breathe.

THIRTY

Spring 1995

Nate was ten. We had been living with Larry and his teenage sons for a year and a half.

I had never been in a relationship with a man like Larry. He had integrity, a protestant work ethic, morals, and drive. He was kind beyond words.

Larry had run an earthquake consulting company in his thirties in Berkeley, which had gone public. With the profits he bought a piece of property and cabin on the non-ferry–served island, Demeter. He moved his wife and three children there, where they attended the one-room school house and lived the homesteading life in a small log cabin on the beach.

Eventually the rusticness of it all became too much and they moved to the less rustic San Juan Island and divorced soon after. He worked part-time at the high school, mostly helping students with work-study and internships.

The first year I lived with Larry I relaxed. I even took naps some afternoons, something I had never done. It was the first time since Nate was born I wasn't holding everything myself. Larry supported me in whatever was important to me. He encouraged me to try new things, too, like riding my bike alone to Bellingham on Chuckanut Drive or riding the Seattle, to Portland route (STP). He was willing to be with Nate when I was working, taking a class, or exercising. I felt like I was no longer in survival mode as our relationship became increasingly secure.

Larry's children were teenagers and I enjoyed taking care of them in little ways. I cooked. I cleaned. I listened. I shared my perspectives on life and emotions, which were very different than Larry's or their mom's.

I was twenty-five and Larry was fifty when we met on the

high school baseball field. I was six years older than Heather, his oldest, and ten years older than his youngest, Matt. The age difference was hard for all of us, but it was the hardest on Larry's children.

It was weird, probably embarrassing for them to have their dad with a woman so young. I came in and changed the way their family functioned. Even though I tried to honor them and their ways, which were so different than mine. My style of parenting, how I was raised, and how I ran a household was foreign to them. I saw the world differently and my cooking was way too spicy.

Despite our vast age difference and fundamental differences in how we viewed the world, we thought we were in love. Larry and I persevered in our relationship and in the blending of our families. It was work. It was only Larry's willingness to yield to me that allowed our relationship to endure. But then, I began yielding too, in a less obvious way.

I was giving up my power in small ways. I thought he must know better than me, since he was older. I started to doubt my own wisdom and deferred to him.

I knew it wasn't right.

I thought he knew, too.

But we didn't correct it.

We ignored it.

We focused on what was working. We were skilled at running a household and supporting our children in their endeavors. After four years I felt we should get married. I wanted more security for my future and Nate's.

Larry finally agreed.

I planned an intimate wedding with only our children and my parents. We rented the *Arequipa*, a vintage wooden yacht and cruised to Demeter to get married at the property that Larry had once owned and lived on. It was a magical piece of property, with water and beach on two of the three sides and a Salish Indian burial site on its point. When we arrived, our friends had left big, white plastic buckets of fresh cut flowers waiting for us on the beach.

June arranged a special bouquet of white tuber roses and lilies for me to carry down the aisle. I wore a knee length ivory dress of cut velvet, hand sewn by my friend Jill. It was a glorious sunny day.

I sang a part of a Judy Collins song a cappella, Song for Judith, which at the time felt right, but it also felt wrong. I should be passionately in love with the man I am marrying, not singing a song about friendship. I wondered why it felt so off. I thought it was just me, overthinking it.

Larry said his vows about two boats being moored to one another, free to be separate, yet always connected. His vows made me cringe. I understood what he was trying to say and I knew he felt it, but I didn't.

I was aware that his children and my parents picked up on the lack of ease. I minimized it. I didn't want to tug at that unraveling thread. I tied a little knot in it and tucked it away. I prayed it would never come loose.

The ride back to San Juan was clear, balmy and calm. We toasted with champagne and sparkling cider, while the sky turned familiar shades of yellow, orange, and pink, as the sun set behind the island. The Arequipa returned us, in all her elegance, married, to the shores of The Mariella.

THIRTY-ONE

Summer 2008

My phone rings. It's Stacy.

"I'm in labor."
"I need you to come," she says, breathing in between contractions.

"Okay," I say.
"We are on Demeter."
"We are at the cabaret."
"Vida is just about to sing."
"We will leave in five minutes," I promise.

Vida, Sonja, and Iris, with the help of Alison, are going on stage any minute at the Demeter Cabaret. They are going to sing "Clara Barton," by Country Joe. Cabaret is at Blue Moon Farm this year, so it will be at least a fifteen-minute truck ride to our cabin. It's a perfectly hot and sunny August evening and there are fresh flowers in mason jars and old vases on the tables, which are set up in the field. The acres of gardens are still lush and full of flowers and veggies. The dessert table is full of homemade baked goods to buy. The talent is creative and varied as always and I'm sad to leave.

We have been waiting for this baby in earnest for at least three weeks. Stacy and Nate have been attempting to induce labor with the help of the midwives, but to no avail. We already rushed over once from Demeter on a false alarm. Stacy wanted Nate to be there for the birth, but he had to leave for Alaska. She drove him to the airport at six this morning and has been home resting with Carter all afternoon. After a nap her labor started, about five.

As soon as Vida finishes her song, Larry drives us in the

big, old, lemon-lime colored Dodge truck down the long dirt roads. It takes a slow fifteen minutes before we arrive at our cabin. He parks and runs down to the beach to prepare the boat for Vida and me. It takes more than an hour before we reach the Lopez ferry dock. It is the first ferry we can catch to Anacortes.

Larry drops us off, illegally, at the beach next to the ferry dock. Vida and I climb up the rocky cliff and squeeze through the fence with our overnight bags and walk on the ferry, which is getting ready to board. After the cars load, I find a red VW bus, with a couple of old hippies driving into the center lane. I tell them my daughter-in-law is in labor. I ask if they would be willing to drive us the mile up the hill to Sterling Street. They agree and take us up the hill when the ferry docks in Anacortes.

It's nine and the sun is setting. It's been three hours since Stacy called me. Blue Moon Farm to Anacortes is a long trip. Stacy is breathing on the couch. My mom, Stacy's friend Sarah, and of course, Carter, are with her. Stacy is trying to decide if she should have the baby at home or if she wants me to drive her to the Bellingham Birth Center. She looks at all of us. She looks at Vida the most, who is staring at her with big eyes because of the intensity of labor. She wants me to drive her to the birth center.

I drive her car, speeding up Sterling and down Twelfth towards the freeway. We get halfway down Twelfth and Stacy says, "I am not going to make it. You better take me to Island Hospital." I turn right towards the hospital. We go to the emergency room and they usher us to maternity. I push Stacy in the wheelchair down the hall. It's nine-fifteen. They contact the on-call doctor and get Stacy in a room. She is ready to push.

We try to set up the birthing stool. Stacy yells at me to stop breathing with her. I stop immediately. The doctor comes in. He doesn't know how to use the birthing stool, either. He's useless. The nurses and I hold Stacy while she squats. The youngish, handsome doctor watches in awe and prepares to catch the baby. Stacy pushes one last time and Canon is born with the force of a cannon ball into the world. It's nine thirty-five.

I call Nate. Stacy is too weak to talk. This pregnancy has not been much easier than the last one. Her iron has been low the whole pregnancy, but especially this last month. Nate misses the birth of his second son. It is not directly about drugs. At least, I don't think it is. Indirectly, all of his absences are related to his addiction. It looks different every time. This time he is fogged-in at a hotel in Anchorage. I tell him Canon is a healthy baby boy and Stacy was amazing. He sounds happy, tired, and disappointed to have missed the birth.

There are now two baby boys. There is a lot for everyone to do. We are going to be busy. But Stacy, she is the busiest of us all.

A week later I arrive at the house to help with the babies and spend the night. Stacy gives me a handmade, green ceramic pie dish filled with roasted carrots, beets, and potatoes with a touch of rosemary. She has taken the boys to the Anacortes Farmers Market to buy it for me. It's a special birthday present.

I cry.

I am grateful.

Nate asks me earlier in the summer if Stacy and the boys can live with us. I say no. They don't have enough money because Nate is wasting it on drugs and his lifestyle. I think his drug of choice is mainly OxyContin. I am not going to help him out. He makes more money than I do. Stacy wants to move.

When Canon is three weeks old, Stacy puts Carter in the backpack and Canon in the front pack. She rents a U-Haul and we load up the whole house and drive to Whidbey. She has been packing for weeks. Nate's still in Alaska.

It feels like the right thing. Whidbey feels like a nurturing and safe place for them to be. My mom still lives there and so does my dad, with his second wife. Nate's dad lives there, too.

Everyone knows our family and loves my mom, so it feels like Stacy and the boys will be welcomed with open arms. They are.

Although they are farther from me, I know they are safer and in a healthier environment than Anacortes. Stacy will be able to develop her massage practice and the boys will have quality childcare. They will make friends and create a community for themselves. After a day of unpacking, I drive up Whidbey.

I make it to the ferry.

I drive down lane four.

I'm almost home.

I breathe.

Nate comes home from fishing. He's long-lining now with his Uncle Scott. He is still spending most of his time out in the Bering Sea.

He is still in a lot of pain from injury and overuse of his shoulder. His OxyContin abuse is visible in his face and behavior. His nose is red, his skin is blotchy and pasty. He sweats more and at odd times. He nods off frequently and at random times. He goes to Everett a lot to see his friend D.J. He goes to the grocery store and returns an unusually long time later. He runs random errands, constantly. It's exhausting and stressful to be around him. It takes a toll on Stacy, too. I limit my time there when he is home, for my own sanity and in hopes that eventually he, they, someone, will hit rock bottom.

Stacy and the boys are easy to love. They are easy to give to and our time together is memorable. When I arrive, they are all wide awake, finished with breakfast, but not quite out of their pajamas. Stacy goes to yoga on Thursday mornings. That's how our visits typically begin.

I put the boys in the double stroller and we walk the mile to Langley. It's the same walk I used to take when Nate was a baby. We get our toasted bagels and cream cheese, steamed milk, black tea for *E*, which is what they call me, as it's short for Grandma Cere. We read books and sometimes we buy them. We make our way into Good Cheer, the local thrift shop and sometimes even the Star Store. As the boys get older I take them to the playground where Carter can run around being loud and fast, while Canon can hang out in the sling.

When Glen is home from fishing, sometimes he meets us at the park. We are talking more since having two grandsons. It's nice to share this baby time with him since it is something we were never able to do with Nate. All the old feelings and attraction hang between us, but he is in a new relationship and I am married. So all we do is talk.

When I drive home from my visits with Stacy and the boys, my heart is full.

Spending time on Whidbey, week after week, allows me space to feel and reflect on all the old wounds of my parents' divorce and my wild, ungrounded, adolescence. As I drive home towards the ferry each week I cry. I can't help myself. Tears stream down my cheeks.

I hate it.

I realize that not only am I probably peri-menopausal, which is no fun, but I am grieving parts of my life that I have carefully compartmentalized. The three hours of driving and three hours on the ferry each week is giving me ample time to process my thoughts and feelings.

Each week I drive up to the ferry toll booth and one of the men who has been taking my ticket for over fifteen years notices my tears. He jokes and assures me that I haven't missed the ferry, as if that's why I'm crying.

Of course, we both know it isn't.

My Volvo breaks down and I buy a used, but newer, Subaru Outback. Larry does not approve of me spending so much money, but I do it anyway. This one act feels like the beginning of the end. It's a separation between us. It's a separation that I have been tucking away, avoiding, not talking about, ever. I have continued deferring to Larry, not about everything, but certain things; issues of money, vacations, wants and desires, and how to solve problems. Ever since he let me adopt Vida, I feel even less entitled to ask for what I need.

Since he is twenty-five years older than me, I have assumed he knew better than me about most things, though not parenting. I have always felt right and justified about my parenting. I fought for many things. At the same time, I abdicated some responsibilities. I am thinking about everyone else's needs, but not my own. I have lost connection with my own needs. But that is beginning to change. I am thinking about myself now, not just my children and not just my marriage, actually my own separate needs, feelings, and desires and it feels dangerous. I feel out of balance emotionally.

Although I am still running, I need and want more exercise. I start lifting weights again. I don't like how I look or feel. I have been eating too much and badly. I want to change that. I decide to do a cayenne, lemon juice, maple syrup fast, as a way to cleanse and start anew. I do it for sixteen days.

During those days I decide to quit cooking, for a while. I take a lot of hot baths because I have the chills and it soothes me. I am overwhelmed by emotions. I need space. I suggest Larry and I sleep in separate rooms. He and I both start reading books about marriage and looking for a marriage therapist.

I call Don and start driving to Mountlake Terrace to see him every other week again. We have ninety-minute appointments. It's hard. I feel like I am going places in myself I have never been. I feel disassociated and scared. I tell Don everything. I ask him to help me not act out the strong feelings I am having.

I don't want my marriage to end; I want desperately for it to last. But I am off course within myself and within my marriage. I read a quote from Elizabeth Gilbert on my friend Tia's blog. It's exactly what I need to hear. Elizabeth says something about the power of simply *beginning to tell the truth.*

I have to become more honest than ever before if there is any hope for Nate to get clean and Stacy and the boys to be healthy. If I am living a lie, or don't even know who I am, how can I expect anything different from them?

It's painful. I have to set more boundaries with Stacy. I can no longer talk with her about the ups and downs with Nate or money. I have to pull away from her, so she can start building a support system besides me.

I hate it.

She hates it.

But I know it's true.

I feel like I am righting a ship and the ship is my life. I know Don can help me mitigate the damage to myself and others. He tells me I can do things differently than my parents did. Whether I stay married or get divorced, I don't have to do the same kind of damage.

I continue helping Stacy each week, but now I take little bits of time for myself, too. I reconnect with Ursula and we go for walks. We talk about addiction in the past and in the present within our families. We talk about our boys, our mothers, and our marriages.

We talk about the day I met her at the hospital in Coupeville as she waited for her mom to take her very last breath. I picked pink plum blossoms from the trees outside the hospital to place around her mother's body. Jeanne lived a life without peace. To see her finally able to rest was bittersweet.

In the weekends following, I meet Ursula at her mom's house to help her pack and sort Jeanne's clothes, linens, plants, and books. Ursula insists I take the pair of unworn, turquoise cowboy boots that she finds in her mother's closet. They're only a half a size too big. I love them. My time with Ursula is brief, but meaningful. It's healing for me. I hope for her, too.

I see Glen a little more often, usually with the boys, but

sometimes alone. When we are alone, we want to be physically close. The attraction is still there and unfinished. There is no doubt we both want each other, but there is so much at stake. We know it's wrong and we both refuse to act out those sexual feelings.

I can't move forward until I allow myself to feel, and say, and maybe do some of the things I have been keeping locked away inside myself since I was seventeen. I stop censoring my love. I share all my deepest feelings with him. I apologize for all the times I put up a wall and blocked him out. I apologize for the ways I made it difficult for him to be involved. I stop telling him what he did wrong and start admitting my part.

It is almost too much for me to feel and think about. But with Don's help, I go to all the hardest places within myself.

When Nate was eight years old, I fell in love with Larry. I really truly thought I was in love. Now I am not so sure. Larry offered adoration, commitment, stability, and a gentleness that I needed or thought I needed. Larry has been nothing but kind and committed. But our age difference and personality differences aren't working for me. They feel like they are in direct conflict with who I fundamentally am. I had no idea I was so unhappy until I started spending time with Stacy and Carter, then Canon.

With them I felt free and relaxed. I realized I had been shut down with Larry. I was no longer feeling joy in that relationship. It had become a business relationship; not a love affair. Up until then, I thought it was all inside of me. But then I saw it wasn't me; it was his energy and our dynamic that had me shutdown. It made me feel like I wasn't okay, like I had to be different than who I really was.

For years I told myself it was as good as any relationship could possibly be. It wasn't until having time alone to reflect on those drives to Whidbey that it became clear. It really wasn't as good as any relationship could be, and he agreed.

If my marriage fails, I am failing my whole family, I am failing my clients, I am failing my community and it's almost more than I can bear. But greater than the burden of hurting and disappointing everyone is my fear of not being true to myself.

I look at Vida as we pick flowers in the garden and I imagine her as a woman, not telling the truth about who she is. I imagine her tucking little parts of herself away day after day, to make things work, to make others happy, to be good, and to stay safe. I see her perfectionism already bigger than it should be. I know she needs me to be messy and real so she can be, too.

All I have ever wanted was to feel safe and to keep my family safe. I wanted everyone to be healthy and happy. I wanted to take care of all the people I loved. I just failed to recognize that I had stopped taking care of myself, which was probably the most critical need.

I thought my marriage to Larry would help me take care of myself, and in some ways it had. But in other ways it changed me. I slowly covered up my authentic self. This might be one part of, or one of the reasons, for Nate's addiction. If it is, it's my part and it's the only part that I can heal.

I dive into what I can heal. I dive into what I can make right within myself. I tell the truth more and more about who I am and about what I need to be whole and to heal. I read Pema Chodron, *When Things Fall Apart*. I do everything I can to be like Pema.

I stay with my feelings.
I stay with what I know is true.

I stay steady.
I stay strong.

I breathe.
I talk to my mom. I talk to my mom's neighbor Julie. She suggests I take off all my roles and practice being Cere. She

thinks that it might help to simply ask myself what feels right to Cere, not the wife, mother, or therapist, just Cere.

I practice whenever possible. I notice which roles feel good and which don't. Being with Larry feels suffocating. I notice what brings me joy. Being with Vida and being her mom brings me joy. Being with Stacy, Carter, and Canon and being a grandma brings me joy. I know my clients and being a therapist brings me joy. My cup of tea in the morning brings me joy. I focus on those things.

I remember my love of swimming and diving. Our neighbor has a heated outdoor pool. It's deep and it has a diving board. He graciously lets us use his pool. I swim with Vida. I dive in as many times as I can. It's more healing than I could have imagined.

I am remembering.

I am remembering myself.

I have always wanted to play guitar, so I find a teacher and buy a guitar. Bob is patient and kind. He teaches me how to play the guitar and sing. He teaches me every week, whether I am crying over my marriage, or my son, or Glen, or I am just a teary mess over everything and he says, maybe it's perimenopause.

He listens, a lot. I have no filter. In order for me to sing and play the guitar, my heart has to be open and I must be completely vulnerable. I finally play well enough to perform at some open mics. I sing and play three songs: "Angel from Montgomery," "You Really Got a Hold on Me," and "Long Way Home."

I feel brave.

I play one night at the Tavern on Orcas. I sing and play "Louise," by Bonnie Raitt at Doe Bay on a Thursday night open mic in July. I sing it in honor of Ryan O., a teenage boy in Friday Harbor who has just died of a heroin overdose. His dad, my friend, found him overdosed in a storage unit. I and hundreds of others, attend his memorial at the Presbyterian church. This could be Nate, any day.

Everything is hard.

Unbearable, really.

Larry joins a men's group, I know all the men in it. Larry says he only talks about himself, but really? I see the men at the post office, when I am on my run, at restaurants, out dancing, basically everywhere. They look at me differently.

I hate it.

I feel exposed.

I can't be at the house after Vida is in bed. I no longer feel relaxed or comfortable in my own home. I walk into town and listen to music when I can. I drink water, no alcohol. Sometimes I dance with a friend, but usually just alone. I am still fighting for my marriage. I am not leaving. I am being painfully honest with Larry. I am trying to understand myself. But I need space in order to do it.

It's scary to be out, to be exposing myself, even if it's just a little bit. I have been avoiding this. I haven't been out alone since I was twenty-three years old. I barely went out before that since I was raising Nate. It's awkward and uncomfortable. It feels painfully necessary for me to explore this part of myself, to be out of my comfort zone, even if it is in a very controlled manner.

I worry about my clients seeing me and what they might think. I don't want them to think I am out drinking because I am not. But I am going through some changes and changes are messy. They are messy on the inside, but they can also be messy on the outside. I have a new mantra. The old one, be perfect, isn't working anymore. My new one, be messy, is better. At least it's honest. I practice being messy and it's working.

Larry and I go to therapy.

It's horrible.

I hate it.

We can't agree on anything. He wants us to spend more time together. To be more insular. I want to be social. He wants to save money, be minimalist and I want to buy nice clothes and furniture and go on trips. I want to play and have fun, he wants to work and be serious. We want everything different. We are in two entirely different stages of life. I am forty-three. He is sixty-eight. It is still unbearable.

When the therapist we see in Bellingham asks us how we would describe our marriage, if it were a painting on a canvas, I can't see it as one canvas. I see it as one of those paintings that takes two or three canvases to create the whole image. I see myself on a separate canvas, yet part of the same picture. Larry sees us on one canvas.

When I try to visualize our marriage on one canvas, I see myself in a corner of the canvas without enough room. I see myself constricted and small. Just by being who he is, Larry makes me feel small. He doesn't mean to. It's just the way it is. No matter how hard I try, I cannot see myself, my true and full self, on the same canvas. I am no longer willing to lie about it either, even if it means divorce. It's the best I can do.

I am hurting Larry and it makes me sick. I never wanted to hurt him. It's one of my worst fears. I wish I could make it different. I think maybe if our relationship could just have a pause, then I could come back. I think maybe if we make the container of our marriage bigger, I could get my needs met in a different way.

The age difference is hard. I feel like a daughter instead of wife. When I was twenty-five I needed something so badly that I couldn't see what I was doing.

Finally, Larry agrees to pause our marriage.

Stacy and the boys have moved into a new house outside of Langley. Nate is gone, but my mom, Ursula's sons, and I help her move. The new house is near Maxwelton Beach and Scatchet Head. It's right by the cabin I lived in with Nate, the year he turned five, the year before we moved to Friday Harbor.

The house is perfect. It's a blue rambler with white trim. It's in the sun. It has great windows and natural light. The first thing you see when you walk in the door is a huge painting that says BELIEVE. It has two bedrooms, a big, open living room, kitchen and dining room and a garage. There are big fir and cedar trees in the back yard and a flower bed in the front.

I am so proud of Stacy for being patient and finding a good house she can afford. Her massage business is thriving. Soon the boys will start Montessori school in Clinton. The school becomes a safe and grounding force in their lives, as Nate's addiction continues to worsen.

Stacy's patience with Nate's addiction, and Nate, are almost as thin as mine, but not quite. She has not given up, yet. She stays with him. I think she needs to go to therapy. But then again, I think everyone needs to go to therapy.

He comes and goes.

He's irritable.

He's checked-out.

He sleeps.

He spends money.

He's rude.

He ignores the boys.

He is high.

He stays.

I can barely stand being around him. I pretend. I try to treat him normally. I see the good sometimes, but most of all I see the sweat on his bald head, his blotchy skin, his red nose, and his fake smile. There is this one smile that he does when he's high. It's too big a smile for the situation. It's fake, and behind it I see and feel his guilt. Whenever I see that smile I know. I know he is not with us. I know a part of him wants to be. I know he is suffering, too.

I haven't seen his real smile in years. I haven't seen his clear eyes. I miss my boy. I drive home from these days heartbroken and grieving for the boy I once lived my life for. The boy that I worked so hard for. The boy I gave everything to.

The drive is long.

I feel sick.
I want to throw up.

I say the Serenity Prayer.
I put Nate in God's hands.
I pray.
I let go.

I breathe.

THIRTY-TWO

Everyday

I say the Serenity Prayer.
I put Nate in God's hands.
I pray for the next right thing to happen.

I breathe.

At the grocery store, I sit in the car preparing myself to see all the people who I know and who know me. Everywhere, I see my friends, acquaintances, colleagues, clients, and friends of Nate's.

My heart races, I dig deep for my dignity and courage. I struggle with what to say. I want to tell the truth, but without betraying my own boundaries and privacy. I cannot say I am fine or we are fine. Nothing is fine. I fear every day for the life of my son, and the safety of my daughter-in-law and my grandsons.

I wonder when I am not there if they have food in their fridge? Does Stacy have to go to the food bank at Good Cheer? When Nate is home, I wonder if he is ignoring the boys. Is he driving them around high? Is he going to get pulled over for not having a license? Will they end up in foster care?

I am in pain every moment. I feel judged, misunderstood, and exposed. I do my best to tell the truth.

I say, it's hard.

Nate struggles with addiction.

The boys are good.
Stacy is an amazing mom.

I see them every week.
I'm lucky.

These are the things I say.
I feel like throwing up.
I hold my breath.

I feel disconnected.
I feel alone.
I want to hide.

I am tired of being strong.
I am tired of being brave.

I can barely breathe.

I pack my groceries and head to the car. I unload the cart. I return the cart. I get in my car. I turn it on. I put on my country station, take a deep breath, and try desperately to feel okay. It's as if I have just come through a horrible storm and barely escaped with my life. Every damn time.

I put Nate in God's hands, he falls out. I repeat this prayer over and over again as I drive the mile down Lampard. By the time I arrive home, I am less about to curl up in a fetal position and more ready to play with Vida, unload groceries, and make dinner. I am temporarily at peace.

This is what my trips to the grocery store are like for twelve excruciating years, over a thousand trips to the grocery store in this small town, on this small island. Each trip is full of shame, fear, vulnerability, and then recovery.

The worst people to see are the parents of Nate's friends. The parents whose kids are doing well. They are in college. They are moving forward in life. They aren't addicted to Oxy-Contin or heroin.

The best people to see are the ones who are living like me. The other ones, who are in fear every day for their child's life because of addiction. They are like a beacon of light. We see each other, really see each other, and recognize the suffering. It is rare though, to see those moms and those dads because they are hiding too.

There is one person I look forward to seeing. I usually run into her once a month, in the morning, in the produce section. Her daughter and son-in-law were once in that Oxy-Contin world with Nate. They are clean now. She has been through the worst and she is on the other side. When I see her, my hope is renewed. I feel understood and briefly, less alone.

I breathe.

THIRTY-THREE

Summer 2010

I am on the early morning red-eye, again—my guitar in the car and my things packed to stay the night. I can't wait to see the boys and Stacy. Nate is in the Bering Sea.

I take my usual route; Marine Drive, Deception Pass, Oak Harbor Walmart for anything Stacy might need, and Starbucks for an Awake Tea latte to sip on while I drive the hour to their house. I listen to my country music station, contemplate my marriage, and call Glen.

Sometimes in the morning he has time to see me, if he's not in Alaska fishing. He's home. I've rented a little cabin so that I can have some time for myself to process the changes. The cabin is in Freeland. Glen comes to visit me at the little cabin in the woods. I play my guitar and sing, and we talk about Nate. We talk about us. I tell him about my marriage and that Larry and I are taking a pause, a separation, but we are still in the same house.

We sit close and talk about that white picket fence we wish we could have had together, with Nate. We talk about what it would be like if we could grow old together, sitting in rocking chairs on a covered porch. We talk more about Nate. We talk about his addiction. Glen is sad, too. But not as tormented as me. He sees addiction as an issue of will power. I see it as a disease to be treated. He sees Nate's drug use as something that should be managed, as he manages his alcohol use. Glen doesn't think Nate needs to be sober, he just needs to be a better manager and learn his limits. I see this as denial about his own addiction.

We talk about Carter and Canon, their big blue eyes, Carter's white-blond hair, and Canon's blond curls. We talk about how much Carter looks like Stacy and Canon more like

Nate. We light up in the same way when we talk about the boys. We share our love and adoration for our grandsons, in a way we never had the chance to do when Nate was little.

Everything between us is exactly the same as when we were eleven, and fifteen, and seventeen, only better. I don't want our time in the little cabin to end. But eventually it has to. We have to come back and tell the truth. The truth is that he's with someone else. The truth is, he will never stop drinking. The truth is, I would never be able to tolerate his drinking. These truths all break my heart. The pain is almost unbearable, but I am finally strong enough to feel it.

We will never have that white picket fence, not with Nate, not with Carter and Canon, and not when we are old and rocking in our rocking chairs.

I let him go, without abandoning him. We say goodbye knowing there is only love between us. I have finally righted that ship.

I walk back into the cabin and look at the mirror on the wall. I have an old, familiar feeling from my childhood. The black streaks on the mirror fall across my freckled face. The intricately carved flowers on the golden-and-black-stained frame are familiar. I walk over to the owner's house and ask her where she got the mirror. She says she got it at a garage sale. I ask her where and she tells me, Craw Road. That's where my dad lives. It is from my dad's house.

The mirror is my mirror from Oakland, on Haddon Road. It's the mirror that I looked in every morning before kindergarten on Maxwelton Road. It's my favorite mirror. I have tears streaming down my cheeks. Everything happening is exactly right. It's not a coincidence that I have rented this cabin. Of all places this mirror could be hanging, it's here in front of me.

As I leave the cabin for the last time, she hands me the mirror.

I breathe.

Two weeks later, Glen tells me he is getting married. I am

sad, but we have healed what we can between us; it's over. We are both moving on.

It is time for my first tattoo. It's the tattoo I probably would have gotten when I was twenty if I hadn't been raising a toddler, taking a full load of college courses, and waitressing three nights a week.

A month before, I'd run into a young woman named Emily, who had grown up on San Juan Island. She's in her twenties now and covered in tattoos. She bought herself a tattoo needle and is learning how to give tattoos. I call her and she is totally willing, actually overly enthused, to give me my first tattoo, if I can meet her on Queen Anne. I'm overly enthused, too.

I make my way up the winding streets and hills of Queen Anne to the address that Emily has given me. It's an old, three-story white house, classic Seattle craftsman style. I want two tattoos. A small heart on the palm of my hand to remind me to always follow my heart. The second tattoo is an anchor. The anchor is for Nate.

It's getting late and I have to leave by six-fifteen at the latest to catch the last ferry home. Emily draws out a heart. It's perfect. It's on my left palm in the middle of my thumb pad. She starts with the needle and I flinch. Now there is a dot on the line of my heart. It hurts like hell. It hurts worse than childbirth. She finishes the heart perfectly. It takes three minutes. She puts Vaseline or something on it and a piece of cellophane. There is no time for the anchor. I rush to my car and race to the ferry.

I look at my red, tattooed palm on the steering wheel and feel clear, grounded, and complete. I also feel a little embarrassed because the tattoo probably means I am just having a mid-life crisis. Apparently there is no way around those, only through them.

I hope it's over soon.

Larry and I continue to live together and take care of Vida, but our lives are becoming more separate. We still go to Demeter, but less and less. I miss Demeter, but I spend more time on Whidbey with Stacy and the boys. Vida joins me frequently now that the boys are older. The grief around our broken marriage is increasingly obvious and painful. Larry likes me less and less the more I am just myself, the less I am playing a role.

Larry and I are holding on, barely. But we have planned for years to take Vida to Guatemala and I finally decide she is at the right age. I am also afraid if we don't do it now, we may miss our opportunity to do it as a family. Despite the strain in our marriage, we decide to proceed.

I have wanted to take Vida back to Guatemala since she was a baby. I have been waiting for the right time. I decide nine years old is the right time. She is old enough to read, write, and remember, but is not yet a teenager. I think meeting her birth-mother and exploring her history and her cultural roots will help her to know herself and make adolescence less painful.

We leave on August seventh. I hired a woman to find Vida's birth-mom and she has. The finder, Susi, has met with Vida's birth-mom. Luisa wants to meet Vida when we are in Guatemala. Vida wants to meet Luisa.

We rent a room in Antigua. It will be our home base the entire trip. We want to meet Luisa and her two younger children, Lisbet and Alexander, at the beginning of our trip. If it goes well, we want to have other visits in the following weeks. Susi will translate and be with us during the visits.

Luisa comes the first day with just Lisbet. She is coming from Guatemala City and has only been to Antigua one other time in her life. Now we are standing in the streets of Antigua, with the sun beating down on us and the mountain on the horizon, watching Vida's birth-mother walk off a bus. All our hearts are beating fast.

She is taller than I thought, maybe five foot six and not

thin, but not fat. She has a big smile and thick-shoulder-length dark brown hair, big brown eyes and dark brown skin like Vida's. She is wearing pants and a black t-shirt. Lisbet has her hair in two braids, has big brown eyes, brown skin, and a big open smile. She is lovely. Vida's and Luisa's eyes meet, and for this one moment we know this meeting, the one none of us thought would ever happen, is happening.

It's a miracle.

We hug, we cry, we smile, and we cry some more. Tears of relief. But no one is more relieved than Luisa. For almost ten years, she has been wondering if her daughter was even alive, let alone healthy, safe or loved. Vida has been wondering too what her birth-mom was like, did she even exist? What was a birth-mom? It is all a bit much for Vida. She is quiet, not exactly sure what to think or feel, just taking it all in.

We sit in our hotel room and give Luisa the blankets Vida and I sewed for Luisa. We brought clothes for Lisbet and Alexander and a photo album for Luisa, with photos of Vida since she was a baby. We cry more as we talk, with the help of Susi, about Vida's life in Friday Harbor. Luisa tells us about her life in Zona 8, in her small house in a more dangerous part of Guatemala. She tells us about the day Vida was born at the little clinic, in the most dangerous *barrio* of Guatemala City.

Vida and Lisbet connect immediately. They play and laugh together the whole time. We walk into the center of Antigua and find a cafe for lunch. We celebrate the mother-daughter reunion and Lisbet's seventh birthday with chocolate cake, candles, and singing.

Luisa invites us to dinner at her home. We accept the invitation and Susi agrees to take us there in a few days. Luisa and Lisbet leave on the bus before dark and we watch them go, knowing we will see them soon. It is beyond an emotional day for Vida. She is exhausted. So are we.

We say *adios* to Susi and walk back to our room. Vida wants me to read, out loud, *The Mysterious Benedict Society*, while she draws. I start reading and she starts organizing, methodically, her hundred markers in a color-coordinated line. It is almost trancelike. I can see she is trying to calm herself. She is organizing her internal world by organizing her markers.

She is finally able to lay down and rest.

The weekend finally arrives and we travel in the van with Susi, a driver, and another translator to Zona 8. We drive through the city and then on a long, steep, single-lane road until we finally see Luisa, waiting for us outside a little store. We pick her up so she can show us the way to her house. Small stucco houses line the road. Some have big gardens, some do not. Cows and chickens roam freely on the narrow, dirt road. The houses are made from cement and are mostly white, but some are mint green and light blue. Laundry hangs on the lines between the big-leaf banana trees in the side yards.

I am curious about Luisa's world. Larry and I speak our broken Spanish and say *gracias* a lot. Luisa's house consists of two rooms. The front door opens to a small kitchen with a table to the left and to the right two propane burners, a refrigerator and a small counter for preparing food. In the next room is the big bed where all of them sleep. There are some shelves and cabinets for clothes and storage. The room is painted a peachy color. She has set up a long table to the left for the dinner. Her mother, brothers, and best friend are all coming to meet Vida.

Luisa shows Vida how to make the Guatemalan chicken stew, *pepian*. She shows Vida how to clean the sweet peppers, by pushing all the seeds out with her thumb. Next they put them in the blender. They cut the onions and put them in the blender, too. She adds hot chilies and water. The chicken has already been boiling.

Luisa's mom, Margarita, brings a huge bowl of prepared *masa* for making tortillas. We go out on the back cement patio with the chickens and the dog, where Luisa teaches us how to make tortillas on the outdoor fire in a big rounded metal pan. Vida is the best of all of us, after special instruction from Luisa. I am not so good. My tortillas either have holes from being too thin or are way too thick. I take photos, listen, watch, and simply absorb everything about Luisa and Vida together. I am not jealous, only grateful they are having this time together. I am fully aware of the mixture of pain, joy, and relief it stirs in each of them.

After we have been at the house a couple of hours, Luisa says it is time to pick up Lisbet from school. She stays home to cook, but the rest of us walk with Luisa's mother to the school. When we arrive, Lisbet shows us her classroom. She is a good student. She wears her uniform with a white button-up shirt and a navy blue plaid skirt. Her hair is tightly and perfectly braided. She is excited and proud that we are there for her.

We take our time walking the dirt road back to Luisa's house. We get many looks from the people we pass. There will be many questions for Luisa when we leave. I wonder what she will say.

When we return, Luisa's best friend and brothers are there to meet Vida. The *pepian* is almost done. We sit down at the big table with our bowls of *pepian*, bottles of Coca Cola and Sprite and baskets of warm tortillas. Luisa is a wonderful cook and the *pepian* is delicious. She tells us that she sometimes cooks food and sells it to make money.

The children play with the inflatable Earth Ball we bought on Orcas Island. There is a lot of laughing with Larry. Luisa tells me how depressed and sad she was when she gave up Vida. She was only fifteen and her single mom–four feet eleven Margarita, could not help her care for another baby. Margarita already had nine children. Luisa is the oldest. She explains to me how she could not get out of bed for one whole year after Vida was born because she missed her so much. Only her mom and her *tia* had known of her pregnancy. She felt very alone. Not even her best friend or brothers knew about Vida, until one week ago.

We are sitting close on the bed, our legs are touching and dripping wet from sweat. Luisa tells me she had wanted to die and was thinking of killing herself the whole first year after she gave Vida up for adoption. After a year of staying in bed, so deeply depressed, her tia came to her house and said Luisa if you kill yourself, what will happen when your daughter comes to find you? Luisa says she got out of bed that day. It was the day she began waiting for her daughter to return.

Luisa is crying.

I am crying.

Knowing Luisa is such a *buena persona* and loving mother brings me comfort for Vida. Discovering that Luisa and I have matching hearts, that we connect on a deep level, and that she finally knows her daughter is safe brings a kind of peace I had never imagined possible.

We decide to shorten our trip by four days. Vida really wants to go home. She is homesick. Three weeks feels too long for her. I decide she needs to have some control over the trip, so I change our flights. We finish our side trip to San Juan de Laguna, and head back on the long bus ride to our little room in Antigua.

I contact Susi and let her know of our plans to leave early. We invite Luisa, Lisbet, and Alexander to spend one night with us in our hotel. It will be our last night together and we will be without a translator. They take the two-hour bus ride to meet us at the hotel.

We explore Antigua together and end the day at a restaurant for a traditional Guatemalan dinner. We walk home in the dark as the children play with their shadows and balance on the church's stone walls as we pass by. There is so much playing and giggling between the three children that their voices hang in the hot and humid Guatemalan night air.

Back at the hotel, we all put on pajamas. Vida and I join Luisa and her kids in her room and climb onto the bed with Luisa, Lisbet, and Alexander. I read books in my broken Spanish because Luisa cannot yet read and then we finally say, *buenas noches* and *hasta mañana*.

We don't know if we will ever see each other again, but we do know this visit has been healing for all of us. It is the hardest for Luisa to say goodbye and I can feel her mother's heart breaking. But she tells me she is still so happy and appreciative that we have come.

We hug.

We cry.

We wave *adios*.

We all breathe.

When we arrive back in Friday Harbor and are in the familiarity of our own home, Vida begins to relax. The very first thing she does is walk down to the garden with scissors and a basket. She picks about a hundred calendula flowers. She brings them up to the kitchen. She arranges about ten glass jars on the table and fills each one with water and a small bouquet. She lines up her orange and yellow bouquets down the center of our long farmhouse table.

Next she is in her room with a bowl and the bag of sweet peppers I have just brought home from Market Place. She sits by her bedroom window and with her bare hands, cleans each and every red, yellow, and orange pepper exactly the way Luisa has taught her for making the *pepian*. She lines the peppers up on the window sill; red, orange, and yellow in that order.

Her work is trancelike. She is processing her emotions about meeting Luisa and about being in her birth country. She is making things right for herself.

I am so proud of her.

I know it's hard, beyond hard.

I also know she is going to be okay.

I breathe.

Fall 2011

Life has been hard, too hard.

Larry and I are getting divorced.

It's final.

We are both still living in the Lampard house. When I am at home, Larry is outside working in the garden or in the barn. At night, he stays in his office and goes to bed early. There is quite a bit of tension. We are both trying, but Larry is terribly hurt by our separation. I am simply sad and worried about Vida.

I am also worried about the effect the divorce is having on Stacy, Nate, Carter, and Canon. I wonder if it will make Nate's addiction worse. I wonder if Stacy will hate me.

She does. One day Stacy, Nate, the boys, and I are in the living room and Stacy yells and screams at me.

"What the fuck are you doing?"

"You have everything."

"You have a beautiful house, a devoted husband and father."

"You have good life!"

Her anger is bigger than I imagined.

I stand in the doorway afraid to speak.

I breathe, and say, "I am not happy."

"I know it's hard, but I have to be honest."

"I have to follow my own truth."

"I can't stay with Larry for you, Nate, Vida, or the boys."

"I can't do it any longer."

"I am so sorry."

Tears stream down my face. I see tears in her eyes. Nate is holding her. The boys stare up at the big screen TV. They haven't see Stacy and I yell at each other before. Shaking, I say,

"I love you Stacy, I'm just sorry. I am doing my best. I know it's painful for you, but it's the best I can do." She can barely look at me as I walk out the front door. I am not sure where I am going, but I know I need to go. Nate looks me in the eyes, as if to say he is hurt, but on some level understands.

She thought it was real. She thought our marriage was something she could look up to. She thought I was someone she could look up to. Now she is not so sure about me. She hates me right now.

I understand.

I'm sorry.

I'm hurting everyone I love.

I say the Serenity Prayer.

I breathe.

At work, I don't tell my clients. I consult with Jan. I decide to wait and see who brings it up and address it only if a client asks.

I wait. Slowly one, two, three clients say they hear I am getting divorced. They ask if it's true. I ask them what they imagine. I ask them how they feel. Then I confirm that, yes, I their therapist, am getting divorced. I, their therapist, have failed at marriage. It's hard on them. At least one client leaves. Others express their understanding, disappointment, sadness, anger, doubt, worry, and concern.

I am letting them down.

I am letting everyone down.

I don't know what else to do.

I breathe.

I worry about Nate's feelings about the divorce.

When he isn't fishing, I ask him how he feels.

He is shutdown.
His skin is blotchy.
His nose is red.
His eyes are glazed over.
He is sweaty.

He dozes off.

I worry about the boys. They say, where is Grandpa Larry? I tell them he's busy. Since we are still living together, I haven't explained it to them. It hurts my heart to imagine telling them. I know very soon I will have to explain. They feel the disconnect. They feel the change.

I wish it were different.
I wish I were different.
But, I am not and it is not.

I worry constantly about Vida. She is scared. She is sad. She is furious. She is losing her family as she knows it. She is living with the tension; the stiff conversation, the awkward passing in the hall, the constant coming and going.

We move her to a private school in the fall. In order to attend, she skips fifth grade and is now in sixth. Spring Street School is just what she needs. It's small and like a family. Everyone there is kind, gentle, and welcoming. She has teachers who nurture her emotionally and academically. Knowing she is in such a good place puts me at ease.

But, of course, Vida is angry about the divorce, too. She is taking all her anger out on me, and it's relentless.

She screams.
She cries.
She is clingy.
She is difficult.

She comes in my room and takes away art that she has made for me over the years. She tells me she hates me. She tells me she wishes I was dead. I am calm. I don't react. I tell her repeatedly that I love her. I tell her she can be as mad as she wants. I tell her, I was just as mad when my parents got divorced. I tell her I hated Grammy. I tell her no matter what she does or how she feels, I won't ever leave her. I will always take care of her. I will always love her.

I know in my heart that what I am doing is right, even though it is painful and beyond difficult.

Vida is angry.

Larry is angry.

Everyone is angry at me.

I keep Vida close.

I take care of myself.

I take care of Vida.

I run and lift weights, but I want more. I need to release all the anger, tension, pain, and just plain grief that I am holding. I check out the youth boxing club on Tucker. I try boxing. I like it.

I work out with the wife of the man who owns the gym, Alexis. We meet three mornings a week at the boxing club. Alexis and I discover we were both single teenage mothers. Her oldest son is now a senior in high school. Her youngest is a sophomore. Life hasn't been easy for her either.

Boxing is intense. She is teaching me. She plans our workouts. She wraps my hands. We hit the bags and boxing mitts fast and hard with our gloved hands. She plays loud rap music. Some of it is Christian.

Alexis is a Christian. She tells me how God worked in her life to save her marriage years ago, when her boys were little. She shares about her relationship with God. She is not preaching. She is open and vulnerable. She shares her heart.

I share too. I confide in her about my divorce. I tell her about Nate and his addiction. I talk about Stacy and the boys. I talk about Vida and what it's like to be her mother and to be letting her down. I share my belief in God and what it means to me. It's different and less clear than her beliefs. I tell her how

much I have had to let go and how much I still need to let go.
I trust Alexis with my heart.
I trust Alexis with this mess of my life.

Alexis prays for my family.
Alexis prays for me.
Alexis is there.

I can't help but feel she is a little gift from God, just for me.

THIRTY-FIVE

Summer 2011

I don't want to tell anyone it's not just the painkillers, it's not just OxyContin, now it's heroin. Everyone knows heroin is the worst, the dirtiest, most shameful drug. Even when my clients talk about people they know on drugs, they say, "At least it's not heroin."

More people die of heroin overdoses than from any other drug. My heart beats like a train barreling down the tracks. My gut feels as if a hundred-pound weight has been dropped inside.

I can't get rid of this pressure, this ache.

It's like there is a shard of glass wedged deep in my foot that will never come out. Every step I take the pain permeates my body, some days more than others, but always, always it aches. There is never a moment that I am unaware of the pain. There is no relief.

To survive, I do what I have taught myself to do over the years when these same overwhelming feelings of panic, pain, fear, powerlessness, and grief wash over me. I pray. Not because I have so much faith in God, but because to survive I have to believe there is some power greater than myself. I have to believe that in some way a higher power can relieve my suffering, if only for a second. If it can relieve mine, just maybe it can relieve Nate's, too.

I have two prayers. The prayers begin out of necessity. At night I cannot fall asleep because I am so worried about Nate. But worse than not falling asleep is when I do. I have horrible nightmares. I awake from nightmares of Nate beat-up and bloody, drugged out on the street late at night or being sodomized in a jail cell. These nightmares feel so real I often wonder if they are actually happening.

My first prayer takes a similar form to counting sheep.

Instead of actually counting sheep, I imagine the giant hands of God, above me. I am below holding Nate in my arms. My big man of a son is limp and broken in my arms. I lift Nate up and put him into those huge hands of God.

For a brief moment I feel relief, and then Nate simply rolls out of God's hands. I gather my strength and pick him up again. I give him to God. God takes him, and for another brief moment I feel relief. Nate rolls out of his hands again. I gather my strength and do it again and again and again. Sometimes I lay in bed for hours putting Nate in God's hands. Sometimes I beg God to take him; protect him, heal him, show him a better way.

He falls out over and over again. He never stays. Eventually, I fall asleep. The next night I repeat the same prayer. All I have left is prayer and my own self-care. I believe that if I give Nate to God, if I trust God, eventually healing will come for him and our family.

This first prayer, putting Nate in God's hands, becomes more than a nightly ritual. It grows into a daily ritual. Whenever the burden of his suffering, Stacy's suffering, the boys suffering, or my suffering becomes too great, which is often, I repeat the ritual. I start putting them all in God's hands.

My second prayer is to ask God for the next right thing to happen. Please, God, let the next thing that happens lead Nate closer to healing for himself and his family.

Many days I do not know if Nate's death is the next right thing. I am taking care of myself. I'm exhausted from talking about Nate and his addiction.

When my family calls, I tell them that I can't talk about Nate anymore. I beg them to please learn about addiction.

Please go to Al-Anon.

Please go to therapy.

Please go to church.

But most of all, please stop talking to me about your anxiety about Nate's addiction.

THIRTY-SIX

Summer 2012

A few weeks after Stacy goes to the Al-Anon in Friday Harbor, she starts going to church on Whidbey. Nate is still long-lining in the Bering Sea. Her neighbor across the street, Cathy, has been taking her and the boys. One Sunday, we all go in Cathy's car to the Calvary Chapel Church on French Road. It's a hot August day and the service is outside in the grass, under the old growth cedars. It's beautiful, but I am not used to church.

I am uptight.

I am skeptical.

I am scared.

Why is this woman trying to convert my daughter-in-law? I am not used to sharing Stacy, not in this way. Stacy tells me Cathy's been coming over to the house and praying with her. I try to act neutral because I know Stacy has to find her own way.

The first week of August, Larry's whole family comes to visit and he wants me to leave the house. It's awkward and it's hard for Vida to not have me there. I stay with Geoff, my new boyfriend, out at his little cabin in the woods. I have known Geoff since I first moved here and he ran the fajita stand. He was young, like me, with a son Nate's age, a daughter, and wife. But he and Mari separated years ago and we just recently began a friendship.

While I'm there, I realize how stressed and tense I am living in the house with Larry. I realize how toxic it has become and how much negativity I have been absorbing. Like a frog in boiling water, I haven't really known how uncomfortable I was.

I propose to Larry we create a plan in which Vida can

stay in the house and we can come and go. It's called birdnesting. I want it to work. Or, I suggest, Larry live in the cabin and Vida and I in the house. I would come and go so he could have time with her. I hope Vida can stay in the house and for us to be inconvenienced, not her.

None of my ideas work for Larry. I have to move. As much as I don't want to leave the property that has been my home for nineteen years, I have to let go. I can't afford to buy Larry out and he can afford to buy me out, with the help of his children. I'm heartsick to lose my home, but also relieved to finally have clarity. I ask Vida, who is almost twelve now, how she feels and she agrees, it is time.

I buy a new house on San Juan Island and I move in with Vida, just days before she starts seventh grade. Vida will live with me primarily. Larry will have her after school the three days I work and every other weekend. We will also take Vida's new puppy, Raina, a chocolate lab-mix we adopted from the shelter in the spring.

The puppy is a lot of work, mostly for me. She overwhelms me with her constant need for walks, her barking, and chewing everything. She chews my brand-new grey Frye boots the first week in the new house. I'm furious and exhausted. But she is Vida's transitional object and she will go back and forth to Larry's with her.

Even though I know moving is the right thing, it's still painful. The grief comes out in tears and in anger, when I am alone and with friends.

I know Vida is grieving, too. She doesn't even want to celebrate her twelfth birthday, but I invite a few friends to sit around the farmhouse table and sing "Happy Birthday." Vida blows out the candles, but her usual smile is absent.

It breaks my heart.

I pray that Vida will be okay.

The boys come for a visit to the new house. Stacy brings

them to the ferry in Anacortes and I meet them there. This has become our routine every couple of months. I'm still visiting them every two weeks on Whidbey. I'm doing my best to stay close, even as our lives are changing and separating.

On the second day they are with me, Canon comes down with a high fever. He is listless and hot. He lies on the couch. I call Stacy and suggest she come up to Friday Harbor and take the boys home the next day. She is quiet and awkward on the phone, like she doesn't want to come. I am confused. Why doesn't she want to come? I tell her, you need to come. Your son is sick and he needs his mom.

She calls me back a few minutes later and says Kathleen, the pastor's wife, will drive her up to get the boys. They will be on the last ferry leaving Anacortes and then go right back on the ten twenty-five ferry. She wants me to meet her and Kathleen at the ferry landing. I hate the whole thing, but I agree.

Kathleen and I have never met. All she knows is I am Nate's mom. I am the heroin addict's mom. I feel judged. I feel like the enemy.

They drive off the ferry in Kathleen's minivan and walk over to my car. Stacy scoops Canon up in the special car-patterned quilt that is theirs when they are at my house. Carter follows, as they all climb in the minivan with my booster seats and the pastor's wife. Stacy is awkward and stressed and doesn't have much to say. She seems like a deer in headlights. I give the boys and her hugs and kisses and say goodbye.

What the fuck is happening?

I feel like a cult is taking my family away from me, like they are scooping up Stacy and the boys and taking them away from me. I love them so much, the pain is almost unbearable.

I am speechless.

I feel like throwing up.

I hold back my tears.

I sit in my car as I watch them load onto the ferry and the ferry pulls out of the harbor.

I have to pull over on the drive home because I am crying
so hard. I call Alexis.

At first I just cry.

"Can you talk, Alexis?" I ask.

"Sorry it's so late."

"I'm up."

"Are you okay?" she asks.

"No," I say.

"What's happening Alexis?"

"What are they doing?"

"Are they going to take Stacy and the boys away from me?"

"I don't know what to do."

"It's okay."

"They just want to help her," she assures me.

"They won't take her away."

"They won't take the boys away. "

"They are surrounding her with God."

I can't stop crying.

I hope she is right.

I cry more.

I talk even more.

Alexis listens.

Alexis explains.

Alexis understands.

I finally feel better.

I finally drive home.

I say the Serenity Prayer.

I breathe.

I talk to Stacy the next day and she explains what happened the night before. She tells me that she was with the women at church and she had just told them about the second DUI she got in the spring. She had decided that very night to stop taking risks and breaking the law by driving without a license. She had decided to take responsibility and to be honest.

She explains how confused and upset she was about what to do that night, about Canon, and that's why she acted so weird on the phone. I appreciate the explanation and feel relieved. I feel connected again. I am glad she is getting support and asking for help from the church and God. I am glad she has help. But I am still leery of whether it is good help. Regardless, it's her journey and I have to let go.

I say the Serenity Prayer.

I breathe.

Nate returns from Alaska the next week. He says he is done fishing forever because of his shoulder and, he is finally accepting that fishing and his addiction go hand in hand. His suffering is palpable: being away from his family, the pain in his shoulder, and the reality that there is no hope for sobriety or saving his family, as long has he is fishing. He has been fishing for nine years. The OxyContin and the fishing go together. Stacy is hopeful. I am hopeful. For a week or two, everything seems to be getting better. They are going to church. They are changing. They are trying to be a family again; a healthier family. They are trying to heal. Nate says he's clean.

But then...

They take the boys bowling one night in Coupeville. On the way home, Nate falls asleep at the wheel. He's still using OxyContin; this is what it does to him. He crashes their Tahoe and his whole family into a tree. Everyone but Nate is terrified and traumatized. The car is totaled.

I am horrified, detached, yet relieved they are all alive and uninjured. Stacy tells Nate he can't see the boys and he can't live at their house unless he's clean.

He is hurt and angry. The church lets him live in an apartment on their property. They call it the Ark. Stacy and the boys are still at the blue house. She takes the bus to work three days a week. The boys get rides to the Montessori school from women in the church and my mom.

I am watching Stacy, her life and her world change. I keep visiting. When I visit, I pick the boys up from Montessori if it's a Friday afternoon. There is still a sweetness between Stacy and me, but it's getting more awkward. It's getting harder.

I am in full support of Nate being out of the house. I am in full support of Nate not seeing the boys. I am still skeptical of the church, but I will do anything to stay in their life. I will support anything that brings them healing.

Nate has been calling me. Heroin makes people emotional and very chatty sometimes. I answer the phone every time he calls. Once when I visit him, he plays a music video for me of The "A Team" by Ed Sheeran. The visual images and the lyrics tell the story of one young woman's night of addiction, wandering the streets selling her body for a couple of grams:

Stuck in her daydream
Been this way since eighteen
But lately her face seems
Slowly sinking, wasting
Crumbling like pastries
And they scream
The worst things in life come free to us

Cause we're just under the upper hand
And go mad for a couple grams
And she don't want to go outside tonight
And in a pipe she flies to the Motherland
Or sells love to another man
It's too cold outside
For angels to fly
Angels to fly.

An angel will die
Covered in white
Closed eye
And hoping for a better life
This time, we'll fade out tonight
Straight down the line

And they say
She's in the Class A Team

He hopes it will help me understand his addiction. It helps. He talks more about his life. He talks about the pain in his relationship with his dad, Larry and my dad. He cries. I listen.

"Nate, nothing in your life will improve until you quit using."

"Nate, your boys need you."

"Nate, you have to get clean," I beg him.

"Nate, it's up to you to change the pattern of men being absent in our family."

"Nate, don't you want your boys to have a different experience?"

"They need you, Nate." I repeat these things every time he calls.

I stay calm and clear.
I am not afraid of the truth.

"I know it feels heavy, Nate. That's because it's not all your burden."

"You are carrying pain from generations of addiction."

"That is why it feels so heavy."

"But you, Nate, you can change that pattern."

"You are strong enough," I tell him.

"I know you can do it."

And I believe what I am telling him.

215

He listens.

Late one night he calls me sobbing.

"The pastor and his wife are at my house," he tells me.
"They are in my living room."
"They won't let me stay."
"They are helping Stacy."
"They are keeping me away."
"They are helping Stacy."
"I don't have anyone."
"Mom, I don't know what to do."
"What should I do?"
"I don't know about all this Christian stuff."

"I know it hard, Nate."
"It's okay."
"Just go with it, Nate," I say.

"But I don't believe all of it," he says.

"That doesn't matter right now, Nate."
"Go towards the light," I say.
"Go towards the good."
"If Stacy believes, then just believe with her."
"Stop fighting it, Nate."
"You need it."
"They need you."
"If you want Stacy and the boys in your life, you have to get clean."
"You have to go towards the light."
"That is the only option."
"That is the only hope," I plead with him.

"What about all the things I don't agree with?" he asks.

"Don't worry about those things right now."
"Just go with all the good."

"Just do it, Nate."

We are both crying.

We are both scared.

But nothing is as scary as what we have already lived through.

It's as if a miracle has happened. Within a few weeks, Nate says he is clean and he is back at the house. He says he believes in God, in Jesus. He seems different. He seems calmer.

I hold my breath.

Nate and Stacy decide they should finally get married. It is all part of fixing what is broken in themselves, in their family, and between them and God. Brett, their pastor, has agreed to marry them in an informal ceremony the following week.

On the day of the ceremony, Vida and I take the ferry at eight in the morning and drive down Whidbey. We meet Nate, Stacy, and the boys at the 11 a.m. service. We go back to their house and wait.

Stacy is not interested in wearing anything special. They both wear black button-up shirts. Nate wears his flat-billed Mariners hat on backwards. He looks pasty white and thin. The boys wear their best button-up plaid shirts. Carter is the ring bearer. It all feels very disconnected and unemotional to me. I feel separated from both Nate and Stacy, but I go through the motions regardless.

We return to the church. Cathy, the neighbor, meets us there, as does Nate's friend D.J. Nate has not picked up the marriage license at the courthouse, but he has bought himself a ring. Brett agrees to marry them anyway. Nate has not done his part and Brett is not standing up to him.

It feels like a sham.

My stomach aches the whole time.

I hate it.

I take photos anyway. I focus on the bright side. The bright side being they are still trying to be a family and Nate is alive, despite the fact Nate's sobriety doesn't feel real.

I have no idea how to explain this to Vida. We agree that it's a little weird and continue through Oak Harbor, drive through Starbucks for warm, sweet drinks and finally make it down lane four to wait for our ferry.

A couple of weeks later my mom is at my brother's in San Francisco for Thanksgiving. Without a car Nate, Stacy, and the boys can't come to Friday Harbor. My mom's friend Julie invites us to join them at her cousin's house for Thanksgiving dinner. We accept. Nate, Stacy, the boys, Vida, and I go.

Julie's cousin, Cynthia, is a midwife and has a birth center on her property in Greenbank. I have known Cynthia for over twenty years, since her children went to the Children's Center, before she was a midwife. Their home is cozy and warm. We feel welcome.

We laugh.

We eat.

We play games.

We feel loved.

It's what we all need.

I breathe.

I want to believe everything is going to be okay now, but December is long. Stacy feels distant; she seems stressed. I don't know if she is mad at me or if Nate is using again, or both. I don't even feel like I can ask. The tension runs high on the phone when we talk and when I visit.

As soon as Christmas is over, Stacy tells Nate he can no longer live with them. He is still using. There has been no miracle. He has to get help. He has to get clean, not sort-of-clean. Clean for real. She refuses to budge this time. She is not ambivalent. She is clear. It is the most difficult thing she has had to do. Nate starts living with some other heroin addicts on the highway near an old motel.

I feel sick.

My heart is starting to change towards Nate. I didn't realize until now how hard my heart was towards him. I had a wall up but don't want to abandon him now. I am allowing myself to feel love for him again. I feel less resentment and more acceptance. I think I am beginning to really feel the pain of his addiction; his pain, not my own.

Forgiving myself is helping me to forgive Nate. I tell Stacy that I am going to try and show Nate more love. I am not supporting his addiction, but while she is being so firm with her boundaries, I am going to be more open-hearted. I am not sure she understands or likes it, but she hears me.

The weeks go by slowly with Nate carless and homeless. I have many nightmares. I pray. I put Nate in God's hands.

One day he stays in God's hands.

He doesn't fall out.

It's weird.

I'm curious.

It has never happened before.

One day when I'm visiting Stacy and the boys, I call Nate at the house he is staying at with the people he uses with. I offer to meet him somewhere before I drive home. I am looking forward to seeing him. I want him to know that I love him, even if he is choosing to use. I want him to know I am not leaving him. Someone drops him off in the Goose grocery store parking lot. I drive up and see him there, waiting for me. He gets into the Subaru and moves the seat way back. We sit in the car together.

He is distant.

He is jittery.

He is grimy.

He is thin.

He's worse than I have ever seen him. He taps his feet and his fingers. He plays a game on his iPad while he talks to me. He's agitated, like he's jonesing for a fix. He can barely look at me. It's painful to see him this way. I can feel it all over my body, but especially in my heart. Still, I am relieved he is here. I think of what Robin said, if he is alive there is still hope.

I say all the same things.

You can do it.
I know it's hard.
You can get clean.
You can accept help.
You can let God in.

I tell him he is a good person.
I remind him of his strengths.

You are smart.
You are strong.
You are loving.
You are good.

He says he knows. He says this is part of why it's so hard to quit. He focuses on all the ways he is good and then tells himself he's not so bad, that his problem isn't so bad. He tricks himself into thinking his problem isn't really a problem. I assure him it is.

After about fifteen minutes of sitting in the parking lot, he is ready to go back to the house by the motel on the highway. I cringe as I drop him off at the house where he is using heroin. I see the swing in the big maple tree. I ask him about it. He tells me there are children at the house. I feel sad. Nate says he is nice to the children. Nate says he pays attention to the children. The children like Nate. He is better than the alternatives.

At home, I polish my collection of new and used thrift store boots. I find vintage owl drinking glasses at the antique store on Orcas one day, when a client misses her appointment.

I eat expensive chocolate in the evenings and I box with Alexis in the mornings.

Vida practices ballet for hours and hours a week. She stretches and soaks her feet in between. Her Girl Scout troop comes and spreads out on the living room floor, making collages that represent their hopes and dreams. On Vida's is a ballet dancer, a map of the world, and a chocolate lab that looks like Raina.

Stacy and I resume our familiar pattern of relating without Nate. One Saturday, Stacy and the boys and I stay at the Best Western in Everett. It has a decent pool and jacuzzi. We watch the Everett Silvertips in their green-and-white uniforms play hockey. We all swim in the pool and soak in the hot tub. I trim Canon's hair in the hotel room as we watch an animated movie about fairies and a scientist trying to save them. We wonder about Nate and try not to talk about him. It's impossible not to feel the pain of his absence as he dives even deeper into his addiction.

My mom drives Stacy and the boys up for Vida's ballet performance, her first on pointe. We dress up fancy to watch Vida at the theater. She's strong and graceful in her bright blue and black tutu. Since it's my mom's birthday, I make her a flourless chocolate cake. We gather around her at the farmhouse table and sing "Happy Birthday."

Stacy and the boys leave to spend two weeks in Buffalo with her family. It is the middle of February. But before she leaves, Nate has seen a miracle worked in Stacy's life. Her skin, which is plagued by psoriasis, has miraculously cleared. Nate takes this as a sign that he needs to give his life to God and try again to get clean. Later, Nate will tell us, after that was the last time he did heroin. But first, he takes a bus to Oregon. He is going to a Christian treatment program. It's called U-Turn for Christ.

One morning Nate calls me from a bus stop in Oregon. He wants me to send money for a bus ticket. He doesn't like the treatment program. This isn't the first time he's bailed on a program. Several months earlier, Stacy drove him to a Wenatchee treatment program. Three days later he was calling me from a cab saying it was too painful.

It was too hard.

He had to leave.

He couldn't do it.

He couldn't stay.

I won't send him money.

"Sorry, Nate," I say.

"I think you should go back."

He won't. I talk to him about being strong. We have had this conversation so many times; I have run out of things to say so I talk to him about when he was a little boy and he used to live in his Batman t-shirt and cape. It was the one my mom had sewed for my brother when he was three. I share a quote I just read on Instagram: *Always be yourself, unless you can be Batman, then always be Batman.*

"Be Batman, Nate."

"You can do it."

"You have the power to change your life." I am grasping.

I give him my love, but not my money.

I get off the phone as fast as I can.

I feel sick.

I want to throw up.

I call Stacy and tell her he left treatment.

She wishes that I hadn't called.

She's irritated with me.

It ruins her day, too.

I never know what to do.

I feel sick.

I say the Serenity Prayer.

I breathe.

THIRTY-SEVEN

Spring 2013

Nate's in Friday Harbor.
I'm exhausted.
I'm nervous.
I tell him he can't stay with me.
He stays with Katie and Andy.

I'm relieved he is not with me.
I still don't trust him.

Nate goes with them to AA meetings. He takes Suboxone, a prescription drug used to wean people off opiates. It's similar to Methadone. He attends church and goes to Bible study one Wednesday night at Alex's house. He connects with people from his past who are Christian. He visits Larry.

He calls me one night for our family's favorite chicken enchilada recipe. He wants to make it for Katie, Andy, and their children. I think this is a good sign.

I want to see him. He comes for dinner one night. I sit with my two children at the farmhouse table and have dinner. I haven't done this in what feels like forever. It's all I can do not to cry. Nate notices a painting of a goose flying that Vida painted. It hangs in the downstairs bathroom. He tells me it looks like a cross. It's a sign, he tells me.

My heart is open to him. I'm glimpsing my son again. He doesn't stay too long, not quite a month, before he moves back to Whidbey. Stacy allows him to come back to the blue house. She is still running her massage practice, taking the bus, and coordinating rides for the boys with the women at church and my mom. She is financially supporting herself and the boys with no help from Nate.

On top of it all she is on house arrest from her DUI.

She's wearing an ankle bracelet. She is allowed to go to work, church, and the grocery store. The rest of the time she has to be home. She handles it with humility, poise, and grace. She is on house arrest for four months.

Stacy is calm and convicted. She is submitting to God's will. She is fixing her mistakes from the past. She is taking responsibility for her own life.

And yet, still there is tension growing between Nate, Stacy, and me. I am always saying and doing the wrong thing. When I suggest the boys and I go for a walk, she says it's not a good time. When I want to read books to them, she tells me it's too late. She is so mad at me. She blames me for everything. But she says almost nothing. She is tense whenever I open my mouth. Nate says I just need to relax and be a normal grandma. They don't need my help anymore. They don't want my help anymore. It feels like they don't want me.

I am not sure I can do what they want. I have a pit in my stomach all the time. I feel like Stacy doesn't want me to be as close to the boys as I used to be. I feel like it's because of the church. It's breaking my heart. I can't bear it. I am so happy for them, but where does that leave me after six years of utter devotion?

I try to find my place.

I try not to intrude.

I fail.

I intrude.

I can barely breathe.

Nate used to say he brought me Stacy as a gift. I said it, too. The same way he gave me that rap song when he was seventeen. Stacy was my present, a sparkling light amidst the darkness of Nate's addiction. She was my firefly. I was like a child, running through the field in the dark night with my mason jar, trying to catch her magical light.

She made the dark tolerable. She even made it joyful. Before Stacy, everything touching Nate was dark.

So, when Stacy is angry with me, when Stacy is pushing me away, when Stacy is shining her light elsewhere, it's excruciating, but I force myself to tolerate her eyes diverting from mine. When she smiles, laughs and shows her love openly to the kids, my mom, Vida or others who may be visiting, I try not to be crushed, but I am. When she turns her body away from me throughout the day, avoids talking or being alone with me, I hold back my tears. Inside I'm terrified it will never end. But outside I behave as if it's just a stage.

I behave as if I understand why she would do this to me. Most likely because she blames me for Nate's addiction and thinks my mistakes have lead us here. She also tells me once that she sees me as a threat to their marriage and that she feels strongly she needs to keep me away. I am not sure I agree with her, but I do know the two of them must be primary and I must find my new role as simply, grandma, icing on the cake, but no longer essential to the cake itself.

I force myself to love her through it.

I stay.
I empathize.
I understand.

It is not her job to be my light.
I have my own light.
Somewhere.

I breathe.

When we celebrate Mother's Day and Stacy's birthday, Nate is late for the lunch he has planned. He finally arrives in a taxi because they still have no vehicle or valid driver licenses, with Mexican food from Tres Amigos and a gluten free chocolate cake from The Goose. He has a lot of excuses for why he is late. They don't make sense.

I know recovery is not a linear process, but I have already been through so many lies, broken promises, and relapses with him, I fear if he has relapsed again there is no hope. If he isn't clean now, after all the years of trauma, help, love, patience, and involvement with the church since October, I can only imagine one thing, it's over. He is going to be an addict his whole life. I may never have my son back.

But regardless, Stacy, Nate, my mom, the boys, Vida, and I walk to their little neighborhood playground for a picnic with the Mexican food he has brought back. We go through the motions. It is sweet, but not that sweet because Nate is clearly on something. I can't stop looking at his eyes; are they dilated? His skin; is it blotchy? Is that sweat on his brow? Is his voice pressured? Fast? Yes. It's all too familiar, what I am feeling and what I am observing. I have scanned his body, his speech, his energy for twelve years now. It's effortless.

It's like breathing.

But it's not breathing.

He is not right.

He is not sober.

We all go along with it. I take a pretty picture of the picnic and all of us around the quilt in the grass and post in on Instagram. Nate has that look in his eye, the fake smile, the beads of sweat dripping from his bald head, and his face is blotchy. I wonder if I am the only one who notices. I assume we are all pretending it isn't true. But it is, he's using again.

Now it's meth, too.

Will it ever stop?

I'm hopeless.

I'm exhausted.

I want to scream.

I can't fucking breathe.

A few weeks later Nate is living in the Ark, the apartment on the church's property, again.

I am reminded of something Nate told me in the last year. I was standing outside on my porch talking to him on the phone. I don't know where he was, but he was in the height of his heroin use.

I had to ask, again, "What do you need, Nate?"

"Mom, I need someone, not you, to just knock down the door," he said.

"I feel like I am inside and I can hear people knocking."

"I can hear people wanting to help, but I can't get up and open the door."

"I need someone to knock down the door and not take no for an answer."

"Okay, Nate."
"I hear you."
"I have tried, I really have," I say, defeated.

"I know Mom, but it's not you I want."
"I just need someone else to care enough."

"I wanted Larry or your dad or Papa Skip to do it," I say. "But none of them have been able to."

"I need someone."

"I know Nate, I know."
"I am sorry," I say, more tears streaming down my cheeks.
The men at church are trying to help Nate. I call Brett and tell him what Nate has said. They are knocking down the door. Now they won't take no for an answer. They insist that Nate go to Maine to a different Christian treatment program called Seven Oaks. Nate doesn't want to go. Nate is scared to go. The men in the church take him to the Sea-Tac Airport and put him on a plane the day before Carter's sixth birthday. They wait until the plane leaves.

Stacy calls to tell me that he's on the plane.

He's on the plane to Maine.

I hold my breath.
I pray.
I put Nate in God's hands.

I breathe.

Life is easier with Nate in Maine. He isn't allowed to call home for one month. None of us have ever gone this long without talking. It's hardest on Stacy. But Nate being gone is also easier. Stacy and I find a new norm.

I visit them. The boys come to visit me. Sometimes there is tension or awkwardness, but I am learning, slowly, where her new boundaries are. She is practicing. So am I. There is still a lot of love. But we are both beaten down from the constant struggle. We are exhausted from the trauma of living with addiction.

We are still scared. We have been living in a war zone, huddled in a foxhole trying to survive. We are trying to come out of it. We both want to live a better life, but the old patterns are still there.

We remind each other of the trauma. We flinch at anything that sounds or feels like the trauma. We blame each other for the trauma, but not really. It's difficult to untangle. It's a mess. We are a mess. We talk about it sometimes. We totally avoid it other times. We try and be honest. Nothing about it is easy. We try not to hurt each other. We hurt each other anyway. We have been in survival mode together for six long years. There are too many patterns to change.

Stacy has almost completed her house arrest. In a few months she can get a valid driver's license and a Blow and Go Ignition Interlock. She is patiently and methodically taking care of everything.

I am so proud of her.

The body of the church supports her, guides her, and continues to welcome her with open arms. Brett and Kathleen counsel her.

She believes.
She has faith.
She trusts God.

I am grateful.
I have faith.
I trust God.

I breathe.

It's August.
Nate has been in Maine for two months.
Vida and I take the ferry to Orcas for Doe Bay Fest for a few days. Geoff joins us the next day. The music is mostly new, soulful, and hip. Built to Spill plays one night in the big field, next to the organic garden, on the main stage. Strings of lights hang on the stage, on the edge of the forest. It's dark and they light up the night with their familiar heady lyrics and sound. On the gray, gravelly beach surrounded by driftwood, fir trees, and the deep green bay, a new band plays. Their name is You Me & Apollo, and their vocals are riveting as the lead singer belts them out in the magical little cove that is Doe Bay. It's what my soul needs.

We camp in our four-person tent on the edge of the cliff, looking over the bay through the madrona and cedar trees. It's hot and sunny, but the breeze gently blows. We fry salmon and sauté Demeter veggies on the camp stove.

On the last morning, while resting on my sleeping bag in the tent, my iPhone rings. There is a Maine number flashing on the screen. It's Nate. I am relieved he is calling. It's the first time I have heard his voice in over eight weeks. The conversation feels formal and tense. I am so terrified by the tone of his voice that he hasn't changed. I can barely hear what he is saying, but it's nothing of substance. He does not seem happy or engaged with the program he is in. It feels like he has been told to call, but he doesn't really want to talk to me. He is holding resentments perhaps that he still can't put into words. He does seem angry with me. What if he is not finding humility or healing?

It scares me.

I lose hope.

I begin to doubt.

Will there ever be healing?

When we come home from Doe Bay, I call Brett. I talk with him about how I am feeling and ask him how the program in Maine works. I give him some history of our family and our patterns of dysfunction. Brett is patient.

He listens.

He understands.

He offers scripture.

He offers wisdom.

It helps.

I grow to trust Brett. I develop a comfort and ease with him that surprises me. It relieves me, too. He is the father of three boys who are grown or almost grown. He has a daughter, Rosa, who is Vida's age. She is also Latina and adopted.

I like the way he is helping Stacy and Nate. I see he is not afraid of any of us. He is not afraid of our worst, most broken places. He doesn't try and convert me.

I respect him.

Stacy flies with the boys back to Buffalo in September. They drive in a rented minivan with her dad and Eileen to see Nate in Maine. Nate is supposed to be in Maine for a whole year. When she comes home, Stacy tells me it was a healing and positive visit. They walked on the docks overlooking the Atlantic Ocean. They hiked trails though Maine's parks and Northwest-like landscapes.

They went to church.

There is hope again for their marriage, their family, and for Nate's sobriety. I am surprised, happy, and so relieved, until she tells me they are moving to Maine. I break down sobbing in the Everett Target parking lot.

I love them all so much, I can't even fathom them being so far away. Stacy doesn't want to leave either. But she realizes, as I do, it might be the only way for them to heal as a family. Even so, I can't stop crying.

I talk to Alexis and Geoff. It helps to talk about it. I feel better. Not great, but better. I do my best to trust God and whatever plan he has for our family. It doesn't matter where they live, as long as Nate is sober. As long as he is healthy. As long as Carter and Canon have a dad and Stacy has a husband. Wherever they choose to live, they have to emotionally separate from me and I from them.

Vida and I fly out to Bangor, Maine in November. We are both impatient to see Nate. We pick up the rental car at the small airport and make our way to the hotel. Most of the leaves are off the trees. Strip malls and fast-food restaurants line the freeway. I am completely unfamiliar, although I know I must, again, be brave.

He is dropped off at our hotel by someone from the church program. He feels more open and loving than he has been in years, but I feel awkward and unsure. I still don't trust him. Vida is also cautious. Nate is, as is typical, a man of few words. I try not to ask too many questions. I don't want to be the interrogator. I want him to share what he wants when it feels right.

We drive about twenty minutes to the church, which is about the size of a high school gymnasium, where he has been living in a portable building the last couple of months. He shows us the farmhouse he was living in first. There he did physical labor taking care of the farm. But they have since moved to the church grounds where about ten men and, across the street, ten women, live, work, pray and learn how to live a sober and fruitful life in the eyes of God. He introduces me to the other men and the man who runs the program. I think I am in shock that my son is now part of another world, one I don't understand, nor am I sure that I will be able to embrace. I go through the motions. Vida and I follow his lead.

Later in the weekend we meet the family of a mason, who has put Nate to work. There are many brick buildings in Bangor, which means masonry is a common trade. The family invites Vida and I into their home and talk about how much they love Nate. The mother shares with me the miracles God has been working, through Nate. When I tell her my story, she is confused as to why I am not a "believer." How is it that I could pray for God to take Nate, but not be a believer myself? I do not know the answer.

The next day Vida takes a ballet class in an old three-story brick building downtown. I want Nate to watch her and he does for a little bit, but he still has difficulty thinking of others, and this is a red flag. He has found God, he is sober, but he still has so much to learn about being a husband, a father, a brother, and a son. I pray he will continue to grow as a man and in his humility. I pray he can stay sober.

We attend church with Nate on Sunday. Vida and I sit near the front in the old high school theater and Pastor Graves stands up on the stage with his muscular physique, gray beard, and lumberjack style. I think he used to trim trees for a living and hard physical labor is part of the recovery program in Maine. Nate sits in front of us, with all the men from the program, and the women sit a few rows behind us.

I talk with a few of the women, stand for worship, and listen to the sermon, which I find uncomfortably heavy-handed and conservative. At the end, anyone new who wants to take the Lord as their savior; is invited to raise their hand. I can feel the pressure from Nate or perhaps the whole church body to do so, but I can't. It would be dishonest.

After church, Nate pays for the popcorn, pop, and Red Vines at a matinee. I don't even remember what we saw, but I think it was a comedy and I remember crying anyway. Our flight is Monday morning, so I return him to the church after the movie and we stand in the gravelly parking lot, full of holes, as the slightest of snowflakes begin to fall. We hug goodbye.

Tears stream down my face as I drive away with Vida on my right. A combination of relief and hope mixed with fear consume my entire body as we drive past the run-down houses and Dunkin' Donuts towards the old bridge and freeway, which will return us to our hotel.

I say the Serenity Prayer.

I breathe.

THIRTY-EIGHT

November 2013

The Maine number is showing on my iPhone again. My stomach tightens. Nate rarely calls me. I answer, of course.

Why is he calling?

Is he using again?

Is he leaving Maine?

He asks how I am and I can tell immediately this is not why he has called. He finally makes his way to his request. Money. He wants money. I have just spent about $1,000 on our visit to Maine, $1,000 I didn't really have. He wants me to buy a ticket for him to come back to Seattle in December.

That nausea returns deep in my gut, and my shoulders and neck muscles feel immediately tight. If I tell him no, he will be angry. Asking me for money is a sign that he is still not taking responsibility for himself or his family. I dread the idea of him coming home. I'm terrified to have anything to do with enabling him.

I explain my reasons. My voice is stiff, formal, maybe angry. His voice sounds controlled, metered, possibly angry. I prefer his anger at me over an ounce of my enabling. Disappointment fills the space between us. There is nothing more to say, again.

After I get off the phone with him I call Stacy. I tell her, Nate asked me to pay for his ticket to come home. I want her to know the truth. She sounds relieved that I am not buying the ticket, but at the same time unhappy he would ask me.

Nate resigns himself to work and earns the money for his ticket. Or maybe someone else loaned him the money. I never ask. I don't really want to know. He will be flying into Sea-Tac a week after Thanksgiving.

Stacy's mom arrives from Buffalo a week before Thanksgiving. She needs a place to live and recover from the stress in her life, so she is going to live with Stacy and Nate. Stacy wants her to come. Her mom can also help with the driving, since neither Nate nor Stacy have a valid license yet. Stacy sees an opportunity to be there for her mom and to give her a safe place to be. She wants to share how God is working in their lives. She prays that her mom will let God into hers.

I don't fit into the new dynamic. I am used to being the mom with Stacy. With her mom living in their house, she will, for the first time since I have known her, really have her mom. I'm unsure of my role. Fear and anxiety swarm inside me and ooze out into all my interactions with Stacy. Before Pam even arrives, I know Stacy will be relieved to no longer need my help. I am the bad mom, now.

Everything is different.

Everything is hard.

Everything is out of my control.

I have lost my job.

Nate's coming home and I'm scared. Their life now feels like one of those revolving doors that one can only enter periodically. I wait *outside* the family awkwardly, insecurely, a bit lost and anxious for my turn to be let in. I wait to be let into a place I used to come and go from freely.

I wait.

The house is clean and quiet. Vida is upstairs on her floor, her legs spread and stretching as she watches Netflix. I've made room in the fridge for the turkey. Stacy and my mom agree to come to Friday Harbor for an early Thanksgiving.

My heart beats quickly.

My stomach aches.

I'm unsure of myself.

I've made my bed up with clean, soft, off-white damask sheets for Stacy and her mom. My mom will sleep in Vida's bed with her. The familiar white sheets with red, blue, and green cars patterned across them, matching pillowcases, and the navy blue car quilt cover the mattress where the boys will sleep on Vida's floor. This has always been their bed at my house and they count on it and know it's theirs.

I keep watch through the wispy, pale yellow curtains with the tiniest blue flowers scattered throughout. I sewed them the first week we moved in from a barely big-enough scrap, I found at the bottom of a box at the thrift store. I used another small scrap to tie it at the bottom, creating a triangle over the nine-paned rectangular window. The door is a vintage turquoise color and it makes the little flowers pop.

Hanging on the porch is the banner I just made by cutting up old, brown grocery bags into circles, printing out the lettering on white paper, and gluing on the words "Be Grateful." It's strung together with black yarn.

The ferry should have docked by now, so any minute, my mom will drive up in her seafoam-green hybrid Honda Civic. When they arrive the boys pile out of the car and run up to the house with open arms. I greet them the same way. We hug big and I help them with their suitcases. Stacy, Pam, and my mom follow. There are hugs, but they come with a hesitation and stiffness. Each of us, excluding Pam, is holding onto the bare threads of our own reality. We are wrapped tightly in our own suffering. Maybe Pam is, too.

The tension and conflict between my mom and me, old and new, is thick. We are both angry. I have no idea why she is angry at me and I have zero patience for it. She has no right to be angry with me. She is the one who has left me. Everything she does or doesn't do reminds me of that. I resent that I have to be the mother, or rather the daughter, that shows up to correct all the brokenness in this family. I resent that she is not attuned to me, her daughter. I don't trust her leadership. I openly reject it.

We wake in the morning unrested and on top of one another physically and emotionally. The boys, especially Carter, is acting out and challenging Stacy's rules and expectations. The boys pull me in, saying, "*E* says we can do it," whether I have or not. This does not help the situation for any of us, but especially not for me. I take them swimming at the health club pool, which is one of our most treasured rituals in Friday Harbor. The sun shines in the pool area and they wear their goggles, diving in the deep end and splashing in the shallower baby pool. They have become confident in the water over the years and I savor this time with them.

My mom and I drive my car to the store. Both of us are stiff with tension. We have had these conversations already a hundred times. We have reviewed her absence when I was two and again when I was twelve. She apologizes and I believe her and accept it, but the feelings I have for her don't change. She resents my anger and distance. She wants more from me, but I can't give it. I resent her inability to understand addiction and change her enabling and codependent ways.

She takes her cues from others about how to behave and dosen't think enough for herself. This makes it difficult for me to show her respect, even though I know it's not her fault. Even though we have talked for years about her own child-hood, being raised by a narcissistic mother who kept her away from a father who loved her and would have cared for her. Even though I understand her pain and grief, I am still the daughter and I want more, too.

So, we sit in the car and argue about my tone, her attitude, and the nasty tension between us. I hate her and her inability to understand and support me in the ways I need. All I feel is her lacking, like an extra weight for me to carry. For the sake of our family, I do my best to lead our discussion to some semblance of truce so we can go back to my little yellow-trimmed house with our organic whipping cream and make a Thanksgiving turkey four days early.

I hate it.

I am exhausted.

I breathe.

After dinner Vida teaches us a line dance she learned on YouTube. We all participate despite the fact we feel ridiculous. It's fun and we all laugh together.

Stacy wants us to do an activity about gratefulness. She has brought a construction-paper tree to tape on the wall. All I can think about is how it might wreck the newly painted wall. She has cut out leaves in brown, orange, yellow, and green construction paper, which we can write on with a marker what we are grateful for; each other, love, God, food, family, the church, a home.

It all feels contrived to me; fake. But the boys, Stacy, my mom, Pam, and even Vida all are at ease. I am the only one who is uncomfortable, ungrateful, and on the outside.

I can barely breathe.

THIRTY-NINE

December 2014

Nate's home.

He's clean.

He has devoted his life to God.

He gets up at five in the morning to attend the men's Bible study at church on Wednesdays. He works construction with Mick, the football coach from when Glen and I were in high school. Mick and his family attend the same church.

Nate and Stacy attend church on Sundays. Certain people in the church, including Brett and Kathleen, continue to nurture them, counsel them, and take them under their wings.

It's beyond what I was able to give them. It's a beautiful gift to witness when I go to church with them. They are greeted with hugs. They are welcomed, included, enveloped into the church body. So many people are proud of them and the way they have opened to God working in their lives.

I have no idea how this has finally happened. Is it a miracle? Is it just the church, these people who went to bat for Nate and Stacy, or is it God truly working in all our lives to redeem us? I have no answers. I am in awe, and whatever it is, I choose to believe in it because my son is here, sober, for the first time in twelve years. Which, no matter what the reason is, I know one thing for sure, it feels like a miracle.

When I attend church with them on Sunday, which I try to do at least every other week, we shed many tears. I cry the most. Nate just shakes his head at me with all my tears. He puts his arm around me. He lets me lean into him. Stacy and he hold their hands up towards the sky during worship.

My favorite part of the service is watching the healing at work between Stacy and Nate. The distance between them used to be almost unbearable. To see them stand close during worship and to see Nate put his arm around Stacy brings me such relief. To see Stacy finally be able to lean into him warms my heart. Watching them look towards the same God and the same beliefs gives me hope. Watching them right their marriage, their family, and themselves is one of the most powerful kinds of healing I have ever witnessed.

I have tears in my eyes, always.

And yet, it's still hard.

The tension between Stacy and me seems to be growing. I am in a constant state of confusion about what to say and do. They tell me they love me. They tell me over and over again to be myself and to not worry about them or take care of them or interfere with the boys. Even when I think I am doing what they have asked, like offering to take the boys for a walk around the loop or going in at bedtime to read them stories, Stacy gives me that serious, tight-jawed look, like I've just stepped on her toes. I walk on eggshells and I am on the verge of tears every minute I am with them.

It is so painful that there is a part of me that wants to let go, to run away, but I won't. There is some part of them that wants me to go away, too because maybe then they could pretend that all the bad stuff never happened. Or maybe it's just about control. I don't understand it exactly, but I can feel it. No matter what, I can't leave those boys. We have our own experiences, rituals, and memories. We have our own love.

I stay no matter how painful it is.

For an early Christmas present Stacy gives me tickets to an Everett Silvertips game, so I can go with Nate and the boys. Nate and I are quietly and awkwardly navigating our mother-son relationship.

I drive down on the day of the hockey game, raw, and bruised. What I feel as Stacy's disdain for me is more than I can bear. I love her so much. We have shared immense beauty, joy and pain over all these years. We used to communicate so easily about our wants and needs for the day. We were on the same team. The way she is keeping me at arm's length is breaking my heart and scaring me.

On the way to the hockey game, I tell Nate that I am terrified she is not going to let me see the boys and that she will push me out of the family and that I will lose them all. I am crying, of course. I can't contain my grief. Nate, for the first time ever, comforts me. He tells me, Mom, I will never, ever, let that happen.

He tells me, "God put you in our lives to protect and love us at a time when we were unable to know or let God in and we are grateful for all you have done, Mom."

It's in that moment that I know Nate sees me. He sees how I have loved them. He will not push me or allow Stacy to push me out of their lives. And I breathe in a way I may have never breathed in my whole life.

My son, now a man, is holding us.

Stacy knows the boys and I have our own relationship. She knows how much I love them, as much as any mother can begin to understand a grandmother's love. She knows how much I love her, as much as any daughter can begin to understand a mother's love.

She lets me come back, over and over and over again.

I am grateful.

I am imperfect.

I am work.

I am exhausting.

She is rebuilding her family. She has to set boundaries with me. She uses her words, her body, and her heart.

She prays.

I am strong.

I am confident.

I am a force.

I pray.

She is strong.
She is confident.
She is a force.

This is her family.

I remember being a new mom and how much I felt intruded on by my own mom. I still feel she intrudes on my role as Nate's mom. She always wants to be involved, to be the savior, the Mother Teresa of our family. I feel that leaves no room for me. I also thinks it's codependent and enabling. So I put up walls. I feel it's my job to stop her, although it probably isn't.

Her input, often simply her presence, I feel as pressure. What does she want from me? Surely, it is something I am not able to give. On holidays she insists on giving me books, trinkets, clothes, etc. that remind me of how little she knows me. I can't stop feeling wounded by her, despite all my efforts. Her detailed stories of Buddhism, or who the latest person in Hospice is, or who she is meditating with seem completely disconnected from my reality. I feel her absence, even in her presence.

It's been this way for me my whole life. She goes away. I long for her. She comes back. I push her away. Despite the pain of it, she stays.

I stay, too.

I feel Stacy pushing me away, but I refuse to go. I do my best not to take her anger personally. I listen to what she is trying to tell me about herself.

She needs space.
She needs respect.
She needs time.

She needs all this from me, as her mother-in-law. She also needs all this from me in the same way a teenage daughter needs it from her mother. I have two jobs. To be a good mother-in-law and to be a good mother. I do my best.

I give her space.
I give her respect.
I give her time.

I stay.

FORTY

January 2014

Stacy and Nate are getting married again. This time Nate has the marriage license. This time it will be at the church, during the Sunday service. It's Blue Plate Special, the fourth Sunday of the month, so everyone will stay and eat lunch afterwards. Stacy orders our favorite flourless chocolate cake.

I hire a photographer. She orders a lacy, vintage, looking, off-white dress. The ladies from church help decorate. I make a couple of banners out of brown paper bags and I print out the lettering, black on white paper. It says, "Nate and Stacy in Grace, Faith, and Love, Forever" and Stacy hangs it in the church.

One week after the ceremony Nate will fly to Maine, return to his masonry job and finish the program. He will rent a house for the whole family. Stacy and the boys will join him in March. We have all had time to prepare and are as at peace as we can be. I make refrigerator magnets of Deception Pass, the ferry, and the boys at the beach for Stacy to take to Maine.

In the morning we wake up early at Nate and Stacy's. They have decided to read their testimonies separately, in the first service to the whole church body and the few family and friends they have invited. Larry, my mom, and Alexis will be there. Nate's dad won't be there because he is fishing. My dad won't be there, either. During the second service, Stacy will walk down the aisle and Brett will perform the ceremony.

Stacy wants to practice her testimony with me. I sit on the couch in front of the window. She sits on the coffee table facing me. The sunlight shines on her. She takes a deep breath and begins reading;

My story began how many tragic stories do, with my parents' divorce. I remember the day my mom left. She told me to come with her. I was rebellious and foolish, so I broke her heart and chose to stay with my dad. I didn't want to leave my room and the house I had grown up in.

It felt safe.

God has recently revealed to me how tightly I was holding onto my feelings. How they ranked most important in all situations. That was a good example, it felt safe, it felt like home, I wanted it to be okay. If I had let go of my feelings I would have seen the reality of the situation. It was not safe. It was not okay. It was a home full of darkness. My dad was unavailable. My brother and I were left to our own devices. He tried to be the parent. But he was full of anger and often threatened my life. Mostly with his fists and occasionally with a knife or gun.

It was around this time that I started to break out in patches of psoriasis, which from that day to this very day has been a source of embarrassment and shame, and which I try to cover and hide. I was hurt, scared, and alone.

I started making friends with people that were also hurt and scared like me; they just happened to be the ones that were drinking and doing drugs. So, at twelve years old that was the path I chose. At first it was fun. I didn't have to think or feel. I just partied my way through junior high and high school. I even graduated early and went straight to massage school.

If only there was someone who understood me and could take care of me... but I was alone with no God and no hope. I was running with my eyes closed and a broken heart.

At that point, I started doing meth and drinking heavily to the point of blacking out. That was when I got my first DUI. I was passed out at a red light (well, it had turned green a few times). The police officer very kindly knocked on my window.

Somehow, through all that darkness and sin, I held a job at a medical clinic doing massage. I was very good at hiding and covering things up so it looked okay on the outside. At work they wanted us to read a book about Pike Place Market and having fun in the workplace. They flew us all to Seattle.

I decided to extend my stay and visit my friend Nicole. She

had been my partner in crime in high school. She had moved to Bellingham and was having a luau. That is where I met Nate. I was full of sangria and cocaine. Nate was the one pouring out the mountains of cocaine. There were a bunch of us using an office upstairs and I decided we should all take the Hell Test. It was in an email I got from a coworker with a list of questions that started with, have you ever...

At the end of the test, the more points you had the more likely you were going to hell. Nate scored the highest and I scored the second highest. We were a match made in heaven. Together we were like one giant heap of sin. And God had a plan to make all that useful. He was mighty to save, and he would pour out all that mercy on us.

Nate knew that night he wanted to marry me. I was just not so sure. I went back to Arizona searching for someone to rescue me. I even got pregnant and had an abortion. One would think that would have been my rock bottom. I should have been on my knees. But I was full of pride and kept trying to fix it on my own with all my brilliant ideas.

In 2006 I moved to Washington and started my life with Nate. It was fast and furious, yet at the same time slow and agonizing. We got engaged and pregnant all in the same week. There was never a wedding. I was very sick my entire pregnancy, throwing up ten times a day. Nate worked as a commercial fisherman and was gone for months at a time, and when he was home he was unavailable.

Again, alone and full of fear, that fear started to turn into anger and resentment. I couldn't stuff my feelings anymore. Nate felt the rage I had pent up for years. This went on for years. Some things changed. I got pregnant again. We moved to Langley. I started my massage business and we had a sweet little house.

There were a lot of things I really liked about Whidbey Island, so it was a little easier to hold things all together. But still the drugs and my rage went up and down. I could manage my life like this though. But God didn't want me to manage, he wanted me to be saved.

On May 12, 2011, my birthday, a friend invited me out for drinks. I appeased her and went. I had a few drinks and made the choice to drive home, and got my second DUI. I then made the choice to be sober. The consequences of my DUI were very high. I got two days in jail, 133 days of house arrest, and lost my license. To top it off, I started finding Nate's drugs and heroin needles around the house.

That was it. That was my breaking point. There was no way out. I couldn't run. I just wanted to die. I had no more brilliant ideas. I couldn't cover it up and the way I felt on the inside was oozing out. I was helpless and broken.

So, God sent me my neighbor, Cathy, whom had just moved from California, and, I had never met, to my front door. She asked if she could pray with me. I said okay. She came over once a week to pray. She prayed the sinner's prayer and I accepted the Lord into my heart.

I was not alone anymore. I had God and he promised he would never leave me and that he loves me, even as the broken, sinful mess I was. He poured out his grace and mercy. Through his word I learned the meaning of repentance. He was revealing to me sin I had never taken responsibility for, and I was forgiven!

I was saved. I was safe. I could finally rest after all those years of running. Cathy would always tell me, do not be anxious about anything, but in everything by prayer and supplication with thanksgiving let your requests be made known to God. So I turned everything into a prayer and God was answering prayer after prayer. Even though Nate was getting worse, God showed me I needed to stop living like I deserved a problem-free life.

John 16:33 says, "I have told you all this so that you may have peace in me. Here on earth you will have many trials. But take heart, because I have overcome the world." I think all the changes that God was making in us were undeniable, because Nate believed. Cathy prayed with him and he accepted the Lord into his heart.

Tears stream down my cheeks. I take in all that Stacy has

revealed. I wish we had been able to talk sooner about the depths of her suffering.

I wish I could have done more for Stacy.

An hour later Nate and Stacy sit side-by-side on the church stage. Stacy reads the testimony she had just shared with me to the over one-hundred people who attend the morning of their wedding. There is not a dry eye in the house when she finishes, and then Nate begins to read his testimony;

I'd like to read this scripture, Deuteronomy 8:2-3, "Remember how the Lord your God led you all the way in the wilderness those forty years, to humble and test you in order to know what was in your heart, whether or not you would keep his commands. He humbled you, causing you to hunger and then feeding you with manna, which neither you nor your ancestors had known, to teach you that man does not live on bread alone but on every word that comes from the mouth the Lord."

When I read this scripture I look back on the events of my life, my drug addiction, me abandoning my family, and my sin. On Christmas morning 2013 I slept through my kids opening their presents. When they finished, I got up grabbed all the money in the house, the bank card, and the checkbook. I had one hope. One desire. Heroin.

As Stacy chased me down the road, barefoot, on Christmas morning, I told her I couldn't stop, I wouldn't stop. I wasn't capable in that moment of choosing anything but myself. As she cried and begged me to stop, I refused.

While the memory is hard to share, it serves as the great pinnacle of God's love for me. He loved me then. He loved me when all that was "good" about me had vanished. When I was nothing but sin, death, pain, and pride.

It was even in that horrid depth of despair, that he died for me. The six months I spent in Maine being discipled to I began to read God's word. I began to love God's word. How it tells us of being dead in our transgressions and sins. All having sinned and

fallen short of the glory of God. And how this is love. That while
we were yet sinners Christ died for us. He died for me...

This was the first time I had ever heard Nate take responsibility for his addiction. It was the first time I felt that he understood his own pain, and the pain he had caused.

During the second church service, Stacy walks down the aisle and they say their vows. Brett pronounces them husband and wife.

This time it's the truth.

It's not a sham.

It's February, less than two weeks since Nate left for Maine. My iPhone rings.

"Hi, Nate," I answer.

"Hi, Mom."

"What's going on?"
"How are you?" I ask.

"I am in Ohio," he says.
"I bought a truck in Maine."
"I am coming home."

"What?!?!" a wave of terror washes over me.
Is he using again?

"The economy in Maine is so bad," he says.
"I think it would be better for us to be on Whidbey."
"We have our whole support system."
"We love our church."
"We have a good house."
"I have a good job with Mick."

"That's great."
"I want you to be here, of course"

"But is it good for your sobriety?"
"Can you stay sober on Whidbey?" I ask.

"Yeah Mom."
"I think it will be good."
"Stacy wants to stay, too," he tells me.

"Okay."
"Thanks for calling me, Nate."
"Drive safe."

"I will Mom."

"See you soon."
"I love you, Nate."

"I love you, too," he says.

I say the Serenity Prayer.

I breathe.

FORTY-ONE

Summer 2014

Stacy is pregnant.

She is sick, not quite as sick as with Carter or Canon, but it's still pretty bad. We decide she is having a little PTSD from the trauma of life during her first two pregnancies. When we figure that out, she feels a little better. Maybe this pregnancy doesn't have to be so hard. None of the bad things that happened during the other pregnancies are happening now. She also discovers if she spits in a bottle instead of swallowing, she doesn't throwup.

She carries her spit bottle wherever she goes. She sees Cynthia at the Greenbank Birth Center. In July, they find out it's a girl. Even though she is still in the womb, they call her Clementine. It means clemency or mercy. This baby is a manifestation of compassion and forgiveness. She is something for which to be thankful; a blessing.

It's the best summer. I go to Pilates at six in the morning and I see a light load of clients three days a week. I swim at Egg Lake almost every day, diving off the dock in the early mornings, afternoons, and in the evenings whenever I have time. Vida and Geoff join me sometimes. There is a new freedom I feel in my spirit.

Nate has to spend a few weeks at the Skagit County Jail to take care of some past convictions. While he is gone, we swim at Goss Lake with Stacy, the boys, and my mom. Goss Lake is deep and green. The water is warm and inviting. Stacy's pregnant belly pooches out of her black one-piece. Her hair is long and blond, her skin is tan, and she has a few little freckles on her nose. My mom's freckles are out in full force and mine are, too.

The boys come to visit me in Friday Harbor for a long weekend. We swim at the pool, play at Eagle Cove, eat burgers at the Hungry Clam, and buy used books at Serendipity. I cook crepes in the mornings and they sprinkle them with fresh lemon juice and too much powdered sugar. I read them extra books late at night in my bed until they poke me and tell me I'm falling asleep. I rub their tan backs and sing all our usual bedtime songs. At the end of the weekend, I walk with them on the ferry and Stacy picks them up in Anacortes.

In August, they all come for the fair and my birthday. It's the first time they have all visited me on Friday Harbor since Nate quit using. It's my favorite birthday. My little family is safe.

My son is safe.

He is happy.

He is healthy.

He is with us.

I take a million photos. I used to force them into family photos because I wanted to affirm to them and myself that they were a family. Now they are a family. I don't have to force it.

It's just the truth.

We drive out to Roche Harbor. The turn-of-the-century hotel, resort, and cabins are all white with green trim. The gardens are lush and surrounded by brick paths from the old lime kiln. The marina is filled with motor boats, sailboats, and extravagant white yachts.

We park at the top of the hill by the cabins and the boys run down the grassy hill to the pool. It's hot, but since the fair is happening in town, there is hardly anyone at the pool. I swim with the boys and Vida. We do backflips and somersaults underwater. The boys play table tennis with Nate and Stacy on the deck. We all laugh.

My heart is full.

When we return home, Geoff has left a chocolate cake and flowers on the kitchen counter. I feel loved. It's my forty-seventh birthday.

I say a prayer, thanking God for this day.

FORTY-TWO

December 2014

Vida and I spend the weekend with Stacy, Nate, and the boys. We go to Stacy's baby shower on Saturday at the church. We go to church on Sunday and a short hike, at Stacy's request, after church. There is a light dusting of snow on the ground. It's chilly.

A friend of Nate and Stacy's is housesitting at the Little Brown Church on the corner of Maxwelton and French Road. She invites us over at two to watch the Seahawks game. Everyone but Stacy is thrilled. She's not exactly into football.

She indulges us though and starts working on a puzzle. We are all happily lined up in awkward chairs facing the medium-size TV. The boys and Vida sprawl out on the floor drawing and watching the game.

The Seahawks win. They are getting closer to the Super Bowl, which is what we are all hoping for. Despite the excitement, it does not bring on labor. Since the baby isn't coming, Vida and I to leave to catch the last ferry. We reluctantly say goodbye.

We drive off the ferry in the pitch black around ten, unpack, and get into bed. I toss and turn.

I can't sleep.

It's two in the morning.

I hear the familiar chime of Stacy's texts.

"I'm in labor," it says.

"We are heading to the birth center."

Stacy and Nate drive to the Greenbank Birth Center. My mom drives over to the little blue house and stays with the boys. Vida and I can't leave the island until the red-eye. I lay there awake, filled with excitement and anticipation. I finally get up at five and make myself some tea. I pack up a few things for the day. I grab some pillows and blankets for the car.

I wake Vida and tell her we have to catch the ferry. The baby is coming. She rolls out of bed, adds some layers, and we put on our Uggs because there is nothing worse than cold feet on the red-eye. It's dark and cold, but I have already started the car and put on the seat warmers.

We drive right on the ferry. There is rarely a line for the red-eye in December. We stop at Lopez. The waves in the straights are extra high and it's pretty windy, but we are on time. We are almost to Anacortes. It's about seven. I text Stacy and tell her we are close. She tells me her labor has let up. She is not progressing.

When the ferry tries to dock, it can't get in. It backs out and tries again. It still can't get in. The wind is blowing hard. The sky and sea are dark grey. The white caps are big. The ferry backs way out to try a different angle and tries again. It can't get in the dock. I go upstairs to see what is happening. The ferry worker tells me that the combination of strong tides and wind is keeping the ferry from docking. I say my third grandbaby is about to be born and I don't want to miss it. He understands, but there is nothing he can do.

Everyone on the ferry has gathered and is watching. We are stuck on the boat, until it finally docks at about eight. They unload and it seems to take forever. I text Stacy and tell her we are driving off the ferry now. I say, we will be there in about an hour. She says, okay, I will try and wait.

I drive as fast as I can. There is no stopping to get gas or going to Walmart. We don't even stop at Starbucks. Vida sleeps and I drive fast. We turn up Cynthia's driveway to the birthing center's parking lot. The big, tall fir trees are all around and blowing in the wind, and branches are falling. The circular path for walking, while in labor, is empty in the cloudy morning light. The little cabin with two birthing rooms feels calm and quiet. Vida and I rush through the double doors of Stacy's birthing room. Nate is there on the couch. Stacy is resting on the bed.

She tells us labor has stalled. It's Vida's first time at a birth. She watches everything intently and quietly. Maybe even a little nervously. Nate is calm and patiently waiting. Birth is a little awkward for him. He is out of his comfort zone. But he is fully present. He is awake.

Within fifteen minutes, Stacy's labor has come on full force. She is ready to push. Nate sits behind Stacy and holds her up. The birthing stool is below her. It's awkward. I can tell it's not quite the right position, but the baby is coming fast. I grab my camera.

We can all see her head is crowning. Stacy pushes, once, twice, three times and Clementine comes right out into Cynthia's and Stacy's hands. Vida's eyes are huge. We are all in awe.

It's a miracle.

Babies always are.

Tears roll down my cheeks.

A healthy baby girl.

She has red hair.

We all breathe.

FORTY-THREE

Spring 2015

We are all hopelessly in love with her, Clementine Grace Penny. She has big blue eyes, fair skin, and the wispiest, reddest hair. She is a happy, easy baby. She is almost always in her momma's arms sleeping, nursing or just hanging out. Stacy is no longer stressed, Nate is available, and everyone's needs are being met.

When she isn't in her momma's arms, she is in Nate's arms. Carter is especially close to her. He is aware of how she is feeling, what she needs and whatever new task she is mastering. Canon gets a new kitty at Nate's insistence and Stacy's horror, just a week after Clementine is born. Catniss is Canon's baby. He loves Clementine of course, but he is more interested in the kitty and is adjusting to no longer being the baby in the family.

Vida is especially bonded to Clementine. Stacy even let Vida be the first to diaper and dress her. If two weeks go by without seeing her, Vida demands that we go, which is not a problem because I want to go every day.

We are no longer living in a war zone. Stacy and I are no longer camped out in our foxhole, a unit, waiting for bombs to drop day after day after day. We are navigating a relationship of choice and circumstance, no longer one of need or desperation.

We have found a way to talk about our relationship. She tells me that in many ways, I had become the mom that she needed and didn't have to push away from at seventeen. So she pushed me. She expresses her appreciation for all I have given her in the way of love, support, and even insight. But she is also clear that unless she asks, she no longer needs my guidance or insight. She simply needs my love and respect. And I can give her that.

We are living in a big world now. We no longer have to make life look better than it is. There is nothing to hide. There are problems. Life is not perfect. But no one is trying to make their life perfect any more. Life is messy. We work to embrace the messiness.

I feel the change each day in my own life by the way my work has developed. My clients seem to be going deeper in therapy and getting more of what they need in their lives. When my clients struggle with addiction issues in their lives, I decide to self-disclose little bits of our addiction story, our family's suffering, and our family's journey toward recovery. I want my clients to know addiction happens to all types of people. It happens to therapists. I hope that sharing my humanness, at the right times, will serve my clients. I'm grateful.

Oh, and Vida, she is part of all that messiness, too. She is a wonder the way she navigates her needs, her goals, and her own self-care. She is a happier, healthier, more integrated person than she was before the divorce and before Nate got clean. She no longer feels a need to be perfect or to make everyone around her happy. She studies, but not so hard that she forgoes sleep or makes herself anxious. She says no to me, her dad, and work when it feels too much. She is honest about what she likes and doesn't like. She takes care of herself and her needs and lets others do the same, most of the time. Her boundaries are clear.

She makes surprisingly safe and healthy choices for herself. We sit in awe of Vida because this is foreign to us. Her adolescence is nothing like what Stacy, Nate or I experienced.

Glen is on the periphery of all this. He is with his new wife, building a home and a life with her. He and Nate slowly heal their relationship. I am at peace with where he and I left off. Larry is also on the periphery. The divorce has taken its toll on him, and his and Nate's relationship is minimal, but present.

Nate and Stacy are leading their family where they feel God wants them to go. They start a family bible study on Monday nights where families can come and share a meal, study, and worship together. The group is growing.

They give a marriage workshop in which they talk about growth in marriage. Stacy has everyone start an avocado pit in a jar. She says sometimes the growing is slow and you can't see it, but that doesn't mean it isn't growing. She had an avocado pit on her windowsill for over a year before it finally sprouted. They both work diligently on their marriage to heal the places that are still broken. The healing is happening with patience and the Lord, as Stacy likes to remind me.

Brett is mentoring Nate, and I can see by the way people in the church respond to him that he is becoming a leader. Brett is teaching Nate how to lead with grace, strength, balance, and humility. He invites Nate to join him in February on a trip to Jerusalem with a small group of other believers from the church. I am in tears as I watch Nate finally being able use all the good I knew he had inside him, as well as receiving good from others.

One day I drive with him to the dump, just the two of us, which is rare. We are in his new white truck, listening to *Take Me to Church* playing loud, but not too loud. We are just a few blocks from their house when he turns the volume down. He starts to talk, telling me about a man struggling with opiate addiction he has been reaching out to. He says, "I had to take him by that house, that one where I used to live. The one you dropped me off at that day we met in the Goose parking lot."

"I took him to that house because he'd said he needed to grab something, a video game. Of course I knew it was a lie. But I waited in the truck anyway." It is painful for both of us, sitting here together remembering what it had been like, how bad it really was. The air in the truck feels thick and time has seemingly slowed down. We both have tears streaming down our cheeks. He looks into my eyes.

"You know Mom, it really is a miracle I got out."

"I know, Nate, it really is. It really is."
I wipe the tears from my eyes.
I breathe.

Afterword

On Father's Day 2014, Brett asks Nate to give the sermon. It will be his very first sermon. I get up early Sunday morning to take the red-eye. Vida is with Larry since it's Father's Day.

It's a clear morning. The sun is rising from behind Mount Baker, which is a soft pink, as we make the turn by Lopez. The early morning sky is a glorious pale blue. I wonder what Nate's sermon will be like as I drive off the ferry, take Marine Drive, head over Deception Pass, and down Whidbey. I stop at Starbucks and get my grande Awake Tea latte, half the pumps and keep driving.

As I drive, I listen to my country station and think about the day ahead. I think about Glen and wish he wasn't fishing and could be here to see our son, healthy. I wish he could hear our son give his first sermon on Father's Day.

I can't wait to see those boys. It never feels like enough these days. On Sunday mornings, before the service, they run around outside, crazy with all their church friends. They make their own cups of hot chocolate in the church kitchen, adding as much whipped cream as they can before their parents notice. They ask me if they can have donuts or coffee cake and I know now I need to check with their parents before saying yes.

I am excited to see squishy, little Clementine and her wispy red hair. She is six months old and I wonder how she will be different from when I saw her two weeks ago for Carter's eighth birthday. I hope and pray that Stacy lets me hold her for at least one of the services. The best is when she falls asleep in my arms.

When I finally arrive I am already tired, but greeted with hugs by Nate and Stacy and the boys. Then they are all off and busy with the details and socializing of Sunday morning church. I say hello to the handful of Nate and Stacy's friends I have come to know and care about. I pour myself a little coffee with half-and-half, not too much because my peri-menopausal adrenals can't take it. I find a seat right up close, next to where Nate and Stacy will be for worship.

The church is filling up for first service. By nine-fifteen, around one hundred and fifty people are seated. The band starts to play. The music is soulful and uplifting. The words are displayed on the big screen above the low, long stage. Nate and Stacy stand, holding their hands up towards God as they sing each word.

When the music ends, there are a few announcements and then Nate walks up to the pulpit. There is a little mic attached to his new denim button-up shirt and his black jeans look new, too. He is six foot one and his balding head is shaved; he has a longish, full, but scraggily red beard. His smile is big. His blue eyes are clear and bright. His shoulders are broader than the pulpit he stands behind. He takes a deep breath, looks down at his iPad, out at the congregation and begins;

While I was listening to those songs and thinking about Father's Day, I was kind of reflecting back on where I was as a father a couple of years ago. I wasn't in a good place. I wasn't a father.

I had all but abandoned my family for sin and for what I wanted to do. But the love of the Father, our Father, broke through my life and my circumstance, and changed my heart and my family's heart, and brought me to this place that I get to share with you. I just want to thank everybody that has known me from the beginning, everybody that I get to meet now. I just want to thank you for the love you showed me and my family. That you were willing and ready to be used by God to minister the gospel of Jesus Christ, and the forgiveness that I was shown.

It is an honor to be up here today to share and minister that same gospel to you today. So thank you very much and I love you.

Happy Father's Day

My mom sits down next to me during the second service. We listen together while I hold a sleeping Clementine.

I'm in heaven.

I stay after church and go back with them to their house for as long as I can. I have to leave by six-thirty to be at the ferry landing in time for the last boat. It's always so hard to leave. It used to be hard because I worried about them, now it's hard because I don't want to miss any of the good stuff.

I feel closer to Nate each day.

He's becoming a counselor to others who struggle with addiction. I am learning to trust Nate, his sobriety, his devotion to God, and his commitment to his family. It's time for me to go. I hug and kiss them all, but especially Nate. My heart is full.

I say, I am happy today.

I say, my family is healthy today.

I don't know if it will last. I don't want to have expectations. I don't want to be disappointed or hurt again. It's not that I'm not positive, I am just terrified to do anything else.

So, I trust.

One day at a time.

Arriving in Anacortes I'm just in time for the late boat. Sitting in my car on the ferry, I eat eat my brown rice and veggie salad with the lemon-tahini dressing.

I have a perfect spot on the outside. I keep my windows down so I can feel the warm, salty, summer air as we motor though the channel. The sun is slowly setting behind the misty layers of the islands. Its rays reflect and sparkle on the water, which is a deep, sapphire blue tonight. The golden sunlight shines through the red madrona and fir trees as the ferry makes its way past each little island.

The rocky cliffs and edges remind me the water is deep. I pause, remembering the summer sunsets on our Demeter beach. It's the one part of my old life I can't stop missing. I remind myself to be grateful that I had that magical time at all.

The few scattered clouds on the horizon turn apricot, light pink, then fuchsia and as the purply, blue sky darkens, a few stars reveal themselves. The sun finally tucks itself away behind San Juan, as we come around Brown Island into the harbor.

Home.

I am almost home.

I smile.

I am grateful for this day.

This moment.

This moment we have all chosen to stay.

I close my eyes.

I thank God.

I breathe.

Acknowledgements

First and foremost, I thank God for being ever present in our recovery and in the pages of this book. Secondly, without the graciousness of Nate and Stacy, I would not have been able to tell this story. From the bottom of my momma's heart, I thank them for their bravery and for their hard work in persevering through the pain that addiction caused in their lives. I am forever in debt to them for all they have taught me.

I am especially grateful to Nate, who loves me despite my many faults and who has taught me more about humility than I ever knew there was to learn. To G.P. for always being a catalyst. I hope you approve.

I am grateful to Vida for sharing *me* with this book, which has consumed our living room the last two years in one form or another. For your constant love, poise, laughter, and insight throughout this journey.

I will forever be grateful to my mom, for her encouragement and endless patience, both in what it has taken to be my mother and in what it has taken to read, and reread, this story. Despite the pain it caused her, she made sure I got the little details of my childhood correct.

Without Claire Bidwell Smith, this story would never have made it to these pages. She believed in my story and in my ability to write it, even when, which was most of the time, I did not believe. I am forever grateful for her patience in staying with me through the process.

To my very first handful of readers and dearest friends: June, Teresa, Rachel, Alexis, Jan, Claudia, Monica, Tia, Lynn, and Kathleen. Without the feedback of such loving, strong, intelligent, and insightful women I would have wondered if it was even worth the effort. At every step each of you encouraged me and told me it was, and I chose to believe you.

Becky Cole, what would I have done without your gifts as an editor? This work is so much more than I ever thought it could be because of you. You saw what it actually was and went out on a limb for me, and you knew the word—Wabi-Sabi—which is everything. Thank you.

To my brother, for reading one of those early drafts and despite our differences believing in me and encouraging me to continue. To R.M., for your quiet but critical support.

Special thanks to W. Bruce Conway for his publishing support and patience, and to Jill Twist for her thoughtful and thorough proofreading skills.

Finally, to Geoff, for reading to me out loud the *Journal of a Novel: The East of Eden Letters* by Steinbeck, for really getting me, and for loving me right through the messiness of it all.

CPSIA information can be obtained
at www.ICGtesting.com
Printed in the USA
FFHW021803160219
50557640-55863FF